UPDATED

MEDITERRANEAN CRUISE PORTS

TRAVEL GUIDE

2024 Edition

Unveiling the Splendors of Sun-soaked Shores: Explore the Exquisite Destinations, Cuisine, and Culture along the Mediterranean Coastline

Jim Baxter

TABLE OF CONTENTS

Chapter 6: Capturing Memories - Photography and Souvenirs 167

Important Note Before You Continue Reading

Unlock a World of Wonder: Embrace the Uncharted Beauty of the Mediterranean

Step into a realm where extraordinary experiences lie within the pages of this exceptional travel guide. Our mission is simple: to ignite your imagination, fuel your creativity, and awaken the daring adventurer within you. Unlike conventional guides, we choose to forgo images, as we firmly believe in the power of firsthand discovery—unfiltered and uninfluenced by preconceptions. Prepare yourself for an enchanting voyage, where each monument, every corner, and every hidden gem eagerly await your personal encounter. Why spoil the exhilaration of that first glimpse, that overwhelming sense of awe? Get ready to embark on an unparalleled journey, where the vessel propelling you forward is none other than your boundless imagination, and you will be the architect of your own destiny. Abandon any preconceived notions and find yourself transported to an authentic Mediterranean Cruise experience, a realm teeming with extraordinary revelations. Brace yourself, for the magic of this expedition begins now, and remember, the most breathtaking images will be the ones painted by your own eyes.

In stark contrast to traditional guides, this book rejects the need for detailed maps or images. Why, you ask? Because we fervently believe that the greatest discoveries occur when you lose yourself, when you surrender to the ebb and flow of your surroundings, and embrace the thrill of the unknown path. No predetermined itineraries, no precise directions—our intention is to liberate you, allowing you to explore the Mediterranean on your terms, without boundaries or limitations. Surrender to the currents and unveil hidden treasures that no map could ever reveal. Embrace audacity, follow your instincts, and prepare to be astounded. The magic of this expedition commences in your world without maps, where roads materialize with each step, and the most extraordinary adventures await within the unexplored folds of the unknown.

Introduction

The Mediterranean region, often referred to as the cradle of civilization, has captivated travelers for centuries with its alluring beauty, rich history, and diverse cultures. In this opening chapter, we embark on a journey to unravel the magnetic charm that has drawn explorers, artists, and dreamers to its sun-soaked shores.

Embracing the Allure of the Mediterranean: A Brief Overview

The Mediterranean Sea, an enchanting expanse of cerulean blue, occupies a central position on the world map, bridging the continents of Europe, Africa, and Asia. This unique geographical location has endowed the Mediterranean region with a treasure trove of geographical, cultural, and historical richness that continues to captivate travelers from around the globe.

The significance of the Mediterranean's strategic position cannot be overstated. It has acted as a natural pathway connecting these three continents for millennia, facilitating the exchange of goods, ideas, and cultures that have left an indelible mark on the landscape and the people who inhabit it.

Geographical Diversity

The geographical diversity of the Mediterranean is a testament to its complex history. From the sun-drenched coasts of Spain to the ancient ruins of Egypt, the landscapes shift dramatically as you traverse the region. The northern shores are often defined by rugged coastlines, dramatic cliffs, and quaint harbors that have provided shelter to seafarers for centuries. In contrast, the southern shores, influenced by the Saharan and Arabian deserts, exhibit arid terrains that gradually give way to fertile plains and lush valleys.

Cultural Fusion

The meeting of cultures in the Mediterranean has resulted in a rich tapestry woven from threads of countless civilizations. The Phoenicians, Greeks, Romans, Byzantines, Moors, Ottomans, and many others have left their footprints on the shores and cities that surround the sea. This mosaic of cultures has led to the creation of unique architectural styles, culinary traditions, and languages that are a testament to the diversity of human experiences.

Unique Experiences

From the cosmopolitan elegance of the French Riviera, where glamorous beaches and high-end boutiques coexist, to the tranquil simplicity of the Greek islands, where white-washed villages cascade down hillsides to meet azure waters, each corner of the Mediterranean offers a distinct and unforgettable experience. The bustling markets of Istanbul, the ancient ruins of Rome, the bustling souks of Marrakech – each locale resonates with its own rhythm and character, drawing visitors into the stories of civilizations past.

A Living Tapestry of History

Beyond its stunning natural beauty, the Mediterranean embodies a living history. Its shores have witnessed the rise and fall of empires, the clash of ideologies, and the evolution of trade routes that have shaped the world as we know it. The blend of Eastern and Western influences, the coexistence of different faiths and beliefs, and the continuous exchange of ideas have contributed to the region's dynamic cultural heritage.

In essence, the allure of the Mediterranean isn't confined to its stunning beaches and breathtaking landscapes; it is a living, breathing museum of human history. It's a place where the footsteps of conquerors, philosophers, traders, and artists have converged, leaving behind a legacy that continues to shape the present. This is a region that invites exploration not only of its physical beauty but of the stories and lessons embedded within its shores.

Understanding the Geographical and Cultural Diversity

The Mediterranean region, far from being a monolithic entity, is a tapestry woven from the distinct threads of its diverse countries, each contributing to its rich and multifaceted character. This amalgamation of cultures, histories, and landscapes creates a dynamic mosaic that beckons travelers to explore its every facet.

Northern Coastlines: A Historical Odyssey

The northern coastlines of the Mediterranean are adorned with jewels of history that resonate with the echoes of ancient civilizations. Cities like Rome, Athens, and Istanbul stand as living witnesses to the rise and fall of empires. The Roman ruins of Colosseum and Forum in Rome, the Parthenon atop the Acropolis of Athens, and the grandeur of Hagia Sophia in Istanbul are just a few of the architectural marvels that grace this region.

The Byzantine and Ottoman influences, intertwined with layers of history, are etched into the cityscapes. The grandeur of Istanbul's Blue Mosque and the opulence of Topkapi Palace serve as reminders of the Ottoman Empire's dominance. The Hagia Sophia, with its transformation from a Byzantine cathedral to an Ottoman mosque and now a museum, encapsulates the region's complex heritage.

Southern Shores: A Fusion of Traditions

Moving southward, the shores of the Mediterranean offer a fusion of African and European influences that give rise to a unique cultural blend. Countries like Morocco, Tunisia, and Egypt showcase the vibrant intersections of these two continents. The bustling markets of Marrakech, the historic medina of Tunis, and the timeless pyramids of Giza stand as testaments to the harmonious coexistence of diverse traditions.

The cuisine, a mirror of this fusion, tantalizes the senses with flavors that blend spices from the East with the ingredients of the West. From the savory tagines of Morocco to the aromatic seafood dishes of Italy's Amalfi Coast, the Mediterranean palate reflects the region's intricate cultural tapestry.

Diverse Landscapes: Nurturing Varied Lifestyles

The Mediterranean's landscapes are as diverse as the cultures they nurture. The terraced olive groves of Greece, where millennia-old trees bear witness to the passage of time, contrast with the picturesque lavender fields of Provence that infuse the air with a fragrant allure.

Fishing villages along the coast continue to preserve age-old traditions, passing down skills from generation to generation. The vivid blue doors and windows of Greece's

Santorini and the tranquil coves of Cinque Terre in Italy are reminders of the enduring coastal way of life.

Yet, modernity thrives alongside history in bustling metropolises like Barcelona and Istanbul. Architectural wonders like Gaudi's Sagrada Familia in Barcelona and the intricate tilework of Istanbul's grand bazaars showcase the synthesis of contemporary innovation with historical legacies.

A Journey of Exploration and Discovery

This guide promises to lead you through the expansive spectrum of Mediterranean experiences. From walking amidst ancient ruins that tell tales of empires to participating in vibrant festivals that celebrate life, each corner of this region holds its own unique treasures. As we set sail on this journey, we will uncover the hidden gems, indulge in the delectable cuisines, immerse ourselves in the rhythms of local music, and stand in awe of the stunning landscapes. The Mediterranean invites us to embark on a voyage of exploration, discovery, and wonder, unveiling the splendors of its sun-soaked shores.

Chapter 1: Mediterranean Wonders - Must-Visit Destinations

The Mediterranean Riviera: Exploring the French and Italian Coasts

The Mediterranean Riviera, often referred to as the "Côte d'Azur" in French and the "Costa Azzurra" in Italian, is a dazzling stretch of coastline that encompasses both France and Italy. This region is renowned for its glamour, natural beauty, and cultural significance, making it an ideal destination for those seeking a blend of luxury, history, and stunning landscapes.

Promenade along the French Riviera

Overview:
The French Riviera, with its azure waters, charming villages, and opulent cities, has long been a playground for the rich and famous. Stretching along the Mediterranean coast of southeastern France, this glamorous region offers a vibrant mix of historical sites, artistic influences, and breathtaking coastal views.

Sights and Experiences:

Nice:
Nestled on the sparkling shores of the Mediterranean Sea, Nice is the vibrant capital of the French Riviera. With its

stunning coastal views, rich history, and artistic influences, this city offers a captivating blend of urban charm and natural beauty. Whether you're strolling along the iconic Promenade des Anglais, delving into the labyrinthine lanes of the Old Town, or immersing yourself in its cultural tapestry, Nice promises an unforgettable experience for travelers seeking both relaxation and exploration.

Promenade des Anglais: A Boulevard by the Sea
The heart of Nice's allure lies along the famous Promenade des Anglais. This iconic boulevard, which traces the curve of the coastline, is a hub of activity and a cherished promenade for locals and visitors alike. The palm-lined walkway offers breathtaking panoramic views of the Mediterranean's azure waters, making it an ideal spot for leisurely walks, jogging, or simply sitting back and absorbing the tranquil beauty of the sea.

Vibrant Old Town (Vieux Nice): A Journey into the Past
A short distance from the promenade lies the captivating Vieux Nice, the city's historic Old Town. Stepping into this labyrinth of narrow streets feels like stepping back in time. Colorful buildings adorned with ornate balconies and vibrant shutters create a picturesque setting that has inspired artists for centuries. The scent of freshly baked pastries and the lively atmosphere of local markets add to the enchanting ambiance.

Lively Markets and Quaint Boutiques
Vieux Nice is renowned for its vibrant markets that showcase the region's culinary and artisanal delights. The Cours Saleya Market, with its fragrant flower stalls and bustling food market, is a sensory delight. Here, you can find an array of Provençal products, from vibrant produce to aromatic spices. Don't miss the opportunity to taste the succulent fruits and

the local specialties that define the flavors of the Mediterranean.

Cultural Treasures and Artistic Heritage
As you wander through the Old Town's maze-like streets, you'll encounter a wealth of cultural treasures. The Palais Lascaris, a former aristocratic palace, now houses a fascinating museum dedicated to Baroque music and art. The Cathédrale Sainte-Réparate, an impressive cathedral with ornate architecture, stands as a testament to the city's spiritual heritage.

Modern and Traditional Blend
While steeped in history, Nice also embraces modernity. The city boasts a vibrant contemporary art scene, and you can explore this at the Marc Chagall National Museum and the Museum of Modern and Contemporary Art (MAMAC). These venues offer insights into both local and international artistic expressions, creating a bridge between the past and the present.

Culinary Delights: A Gastronomic Journey
Nice's culinary scene is as diverse as its cultural heritage. Sidewalk cafes and bistros offer a taste of the city's vibrant food culture. Indulge in a traditional socca—a savory pancake made from chickpea flour—sold by street vendors. The local Nicoise salad, with fresh vegetables, olives, and anchovies, captures the essence of Mediterranean flavors. For a sweet finish, savor a slice of tarte aux citrons, a lemon tart that showcases the region's love for citrus.

Sunsets and Seascapes
As the sun begins its descent, the Promenade des Anglais transforms into an ideal location to witness the magic of a Mediterranean sunset. The changing hues of the sky reflect on the tranquil waters, creating a captivating and romantic

atmosphere. Locals and visitors gather along the promenade to witness this daily spectacle—a moment of serenity and beauty that captures the essence of Nice.

Nice encapsulates the essence of the French Riviera with its blend of coastal allure, historical charm, and artistic vibrancy. Whether you're leisurely strolling along the promenade, exploring the enchanting Old Town, or savoring the flavors of its cuisine, Nice offers an immersive experience that lingers in the hearts and memories of those who are fortunate enough to visit.

Cannes:

Nestled along the picturesque French Riviera, Cannes emerges as an epitome of elegance, renowned not only for its iconic film festival but also for its timeless allure and captivating attractions. Steeped in a rich history and an atmosphere of luxury, Cannes is a destination that beckons travelers with its blend of cultural heritage, designer boutiques, and breathtaking landscapes.

The Palais des Festivals and the Red Carpet Experience:

The beating heart of Cannes' cinematic legacy resides within the Palais des Festivals et des Congrès. This prestigious venue hosts the internationally acclaimed Cannes Film Festival, an event that transforms the city into a hub of celebrity, creativity, and cinema. As you approach the Palais, you can almost feel the energy of the countless artists who have walked the hallowed red carpet. Imagine the anticipation and excitement that fills the air as filmmakers, actors, and cinephiles gather to celebrate the art of storytelling.

During the festival, the Palais becomes a theater of dreams, screening a diverse array of films from around the world.

While attending a film premiere here is a coveted experience, even strolling by the Palais and taking a moment to absorb its aura is a privilege. The red carpet itself, bathed in the glow of camera flashes and surrounded by the buzz of anticipation, is a symbol of glamour that has transcended generations.

La Croisette: Where Fashion and Luxury Converge:
Adjacent to the sparkling Mediterranean Sea lies La Croisette, a boulevard that epitomizes luxury and style. This iconic promenade stretches along the coastline, offering a panoramic view of the azure waters and pristine beaches. The palm-lined street is flanked by high-end boutiques, upscale hotels, and exclusive restaurants, creating an ambiance that exudes opulence.

For fashion enthusiasts and connoisseurs of luxury, La Croisette is a paradise. Renowned designer boutiques line the street, showcasing the latest collections from global fashion houses. Chanel, Louis Vuitton, and Dior are just a few of the names that grace this fashionable stretch. Whether you're indulging in retail therapy or simply admiring the window displays, La Croisette invites you to immerse yourself in the world of haute couture and refinement.

Le Suquet: The Old Quarter's Timeless Charms:
Beyond the glitz and glamour lies Le Suquet, Cannes' historic old quarter. Perched atop a hill overlooking the bay, Le Suquet transports visitors back in time with its cobbled streets, charming alleyways, and medieval architecture. The contrast between the modernity of La Croisette and the rustic beauty of Le Suquet creates a harmonious balance that defines Cannes' character.

Climbing the winding streets of Le Suquet rewards you with not only a glimpse into Cannes' past but also with stunning panoramic vistas. From the vantage point atop the hill, you can take in the sweeping views of the Mediterranean, the harbor filled with yachts, and the mosaic of rooftops below. At sunset, the scene becomes an artist's palette, awash with warm hues that cast a magical glow over the city.

Cannes Beyond the Surface: Insider Tips:

- Marché Forville: Immerse yourself in local life at the Forville Market, where vibrant displays of fresh produce, regional specialties, and artisanal goods await.
- Île Sainte-Marguerite: Take a short boat ride to this tranquil island known for its natural beauty and the historic Fort Royal, where the enigmatic Man in the Iron Mask was imprisoned.
- Lérins Islands: Explore the Lérins Islands, a pair of idyllic islands just off the coast of Cannes, offering hiking trails, pristine beaches, and a sense of serenity.

Cannes' charm extends far beyond its cinematic reputation. It's a place where history, luxury, and authenticity converge, inviting travelers to explore its layers and discover the stories that have shaped its identity. Whether you're walking the red carpet, indulging in haute couture, or savoring the timeless beauty of its old quarter, Cannes promises an experience that lingers in the heart and memory long after you've departed its shores.

Antibes:

Nestled along the sun-kissed shores of the French Riviera, Antibes is a gem that seamlessly marries its rich history with modern elegance. This charming town exudes an irresistible allure, with its stunning harbor brimming with opulent yachts and a cultural scene that includes the renowned Picasso Museum. As you step into Antibes, you'll find yourself transported to a world where the past blends harmoniously with the present.

A Glimpse into History:

Antibes' roots can be traced back to ancient times, when it was known as "Antipolis" in Greek. Its strategic location along the Mediterranean coast made it a coveted port for various civilizations, including the Greeks, Romans, and even the Byzantines. The remnants of its history are woven into the town's fabric, evident in its historic buildings, cobblestone streets, and ancient fortifications.

The Enchanting Harbor:

One of Antibes' most captivating features is its picturesque harbor, known as Port Vauban. This deep natural harbor has served as a haven for sailors and traders for centuries. Today, it has transformed into a playground for the world's elite, with luxurious yachts and sailboats dotting the azure waters. Walking along the promenade that lines the harbor, you'll be treated to breathtaking views of the Mediterranean and the imposing yachts that adorn its waters.

A Glimpse into Picasso's World:

The Picasso Museum in Antibes stands as a testament to the town's artistic spirit and cultural significance. Housed within the historic Château Grimaldi, a former fortress that dates back to the 12th century, the museum showcases an impressive collection of artworks by the legendary Spanish artist, Pablo Picasso. As you explore the museum's halls, you'll encounter an array of paintings, sculptures, ceramics, and drawings that offer insights into Picasso's creative evolution and his deep connection to the town.

Picasso's time in Antibes was marked by prolific creativity, and the museum's collection includes pieces that were created during his stay. The fusion of Picasso's art with the historical backdrop of the fortress creates a unique and immersive experience for visitors. The museum also features works by other artists, making it a diverse artistic haven that celebrates both established and emerging talents.

Exploring Antibes' Charms:
Beyond its harbor and museum, Antibes offers a plethora of captivating experiences:

- Old Town (Vieil Antibes): Wander through the maze-like streets of the Old Town, where you'll encounter vibrant markets, artisan shops, and charming cafes. The architecture here reflects a blend of Mediterranean and Provençal styles.

- Cap d'Antibes: Embark on a scenic walk along the coastline of Cap d'Antibes, a peninsula that offers stunning vistas and hidden coves. The walk is punctuated by the iconic lighthouse and the Villa Eilenroc, a historic mansion surrounded by lush gardens.

- Marché Provençal: Immerse yourself in the vibrant atmosphere of Antibes' Provençal Market. Here, you can savor the aromas of fresh produce, local cheeses, and fragrant flowers. It's an ideal place to pick up ingredients for a picnic or to create your own Mediterranean-inspired meal.

Savoring the Local Flavors:
Antibes' culinary scene is a feast for the senses. The town's proximity to the sea ensures that seafood takes center stage on many menus. Indulge in delicacies such as bouillabaisse, a traditional Provençal fish stew, and seafood platters that feature the freshest catches from the Mediterranean.

Local Tips:

- Visit Off-Peak: Antibes is at its best during the shoulder seasons of spring and fall when the weather is pleasant, and the crowds are fewer.
- Take a Stroll: Walking is the best way to explore Antibes' intricate streets and alleys, allowing you to uncover hidden corners and unexpected delights.
- Artistic Inspirations: Channel your inner artist and capture the town's beauty through sketching or photography, drawing inspiration from the landscapes that inspired Picasso himself.

Antibes is a town that weaves together the threads of history, art, and luxury into a tapestry of allure. Its historic charm, combined with the modern indulgences of its harbor, creates an enchanting destination that offers a glimpse into the heart of the French Riviera. Whether you're captivated by its artistic heritage, drawn to its maritime elegance, or simply seeking a tranquil escape by the sea, Antibes promises an experience that will linger in your memories long after you've left its shores.

Monaco:

Nestled along the Mediterranean coastline, Monaco stands as a captivating enclave that boasts opulence, glamour, and cultural richness. While technically not a part of France, this sovereign city-state is a glittering gem on the French Riviera, renowned for its stunning architecture, elite lifestyle, and world-class attractions. From the grandeur of the Monte Carlo Casino to the historical significance of the Prince's Palace, and the adrenaline-fueled excitement of the Formula 1 Grand Prix circuit, Monaco offers an extraordinary tapestry of experiences that should not be missed.

Exploring the Opulent Monte Carlo Casino:
The Monte Carlo Casino is more than just a gambling venue; it's a symbol of extravagance and elegance that has left an indelible mark on popular culture. As you approach the casino's ornate façade, adorned with sculptures and intricate detailing, you'll immediately feel the allure of the Belle Époque era. Step inside, and you'll find yourself surrounded by lavish interiors, chandeliers, and art that exude luxury.

Gaming and Entertainment:
While the casino's gaming rooms are known for their high-stakes gambling, the Casino de Monte-Carlo is equally famous for its entertainment offerings. Elegant halls host ballet performances, opera concerts, and classical music recitals, providing a taste of sophistication for those seeking culture beyond the casino floor.

Marveling at the Prince's Palace:
Perched atop a rocky hill, the Prince's Palace of Monaco is a testament to centuries of history and dynastic rule. This fortified palace has been the residence of the Grimaldi family since the 13th century, making it one of the oldest monarchies in the world. The Changing of the Guard ceremony is a spectacle that draws visitors to witness the precision and pageantry of the palace's sentinels.

State Apartments and Historical Exhibits:
Visitors can explore the State Apartments, which are adorned with ornate décor, tapestries, and artwork that reflect the palace's regal history. The palace also houses the Napoleon Museum, which showcases artifacts from Napoleon Bonaparte's reign and his ties to the principality.

Soaking in the Atmosphere of the Formula 1 Grand Prix Circuit:

Monaco is synonymous with the exhilarating Formula 1 Grand Prix circuit that winds its way through the streets of the city. Each year, the streets transform into a racetrack that challenges the skills of the world's best drivers. The Monaco Grand Prix is not only a high-speed sporting event but also a cultural phenomenon that attracts enthusiasts from around the globe.

Unique Challenges and Experiences:

The Monaco Grand Prix circuit is known for its tight corners, elevation changes, and proximity to barriers, making it one of the most demanding tracks in Formula 1. Fans can experience the excitement up close, watching as cars navigate the iconic hairpin turn, race along the tunnel, and speed through the harbor section.

Luxury Living and High Society:

Monaco's reputation for luxury extends beyond its attractions; it's a way of life for its residents and visitors alike. High-end boutiques line the streets, offering the latest in fashion and jewelry from renowned designers. Exclusive restaurants and cafes provide exquisite dining experiences, with many overlooking the azure waters of the Mediterranean.

Sustainable Initiatives and Modernity:

Beyond its lavish lifestyle, Monaco is also making strides in sustainability and modernity. The principality has embraced initiatives to promote eco-friendly practices, including solar energy and sustainable transportation options. The Fontvieille district, reclaimed from the sea, showcases contemporary architecture and innovative urban planning.

Monaco's allure lies in its ability to seamlessly blend centuries-old traditions with contemporary glamour. Whether you're admiring the intricate details of the Monte Carlo Casino, immersing yourself in the historical significance of the Prince's Palace, or feeling the rush of the Formula 1 Grand Prix circuit, Monaco offers a sensory experience that is nothing short of extraordinary. It's a place where the past and present coexist harmoniously, inviting visitors to explore its diverse offerings and become a part of its unique story of luxury and grandeur.

Eze:

Perched gracefully on a dramatic hilltop overlooking the azure expanse of the Mediterranean Sea, the village of Eze is a hidden gem nestled between Nice and Monaco on the French Riviera. With its medieval charm, winding alleys, and stunning views, Eze offers an enchanting escape that invites visitors to step back in time while enjoying a contemporary blend of art, history, and natural beauty.

A Picturesque Journey: Ascending to Eze

To reach Eze, one embarks on a picturesque ascent, winding through narrow roads that gradually lead to the village's lofty vantage point. The journey itself is a preview of the breathtaking views to come. As travelers ascend, the sweeping panorama of the Mediterranean coastline unfolds, creating a sense of anticipation for the delights that await at the summit.

Narrow Alleys and Medieval Splendor

Upon arrival in Eze, visitors are greeted by a labyrinth of narrow, cobblestone alleys that wind their way through the heart of the village. These charming passageways, lined with ancient stone houses adorned with colorful shutters and vibrant bougainvillaea, exude an atmosphere of medieval enchantment.

As you meander through the alleys, it's easy to lose track of time, as each corner reveals a new discovery. Quaint boutiques, art galleries, and craft shops beckon with their unique offerings. From handmade jewelry to intricate ceramics, Eze is a haven for those seeking one-of-a-kind treasures. The absence of vehicular traffic only enhances the village's serenity, allowing visitors to immerse themselves fully in its rustic charm.

Jardin Exotique: A Botanical Masterpiece

One of Eze's crown jewels is the Jardin Exotique, a meticulously landscaped garden that showcases a captivating collection of succulents and rare plants from around the world. The garden's location on a rocky plateau offers an elevated perspective that accentuates the mesmerizing beauty of the Mediterranean panorama.

Wandering through the Jardin Exotique, visitors encounter an array of plant species thriving in harmony with the rocky terrain. Giant cacti, agave plants, and other succulents create a tapestry of textures and colors against the backdrop of the sea. The garden's pathways lead to vantage points that offer spellbinding views, allowing visitors to appreciate the convergence of nature's wonders and human creativity.

Artistic Inspirations: Eze's Creative Community

Eze has long been a muse for artists, writers, and creatives drawn to its ethereal landscapes and timeless ambiance. The village has fostered a vibrant artistic community that draws inspiration from the surroundings. Visitors can engage with local artists, observe their work, and even partake in workshops that explore various creative mediums.

Many of the art galleries and studios in Eze provide glimpses into the creative process, showcasing paintings, sculptures, and crafts that capture the essence of the village and its surroundings. The combination of Eze's natural beauty and the artistic energy that permeates its streets creates an environment that encourages both introspection and expression.

Culinary Delights and Epicurean Adventures

Eze's captivating atmosphere extends to its culinary offerings, which blend Provençal flavors with innovative gastronomy. The village boasts a selection of gourmet restaurants that provide not only delectable cuisine but also spectacular views of the Mediterranean. Dining in Eze is an experience that engages all the senses, from the aroma of freshly prepared dishes to the visual feast of the coastal landscape stretching below.

Visitors have the opportunity to savor traditional Mediterranean dishes made from locally sourced ingredients, as well as contemporary interpretations that reflect the region's culinary evolution. Whether indulging in a leisurely meal or enjoying a cafe au lait on a sun-dappled terrace, Eze's dining options offer an exquisite fusion of flavors and ambiance.

Capturing Timeless Memories

Eze's blend of natural beauty, artistic spirit, and historical charm creates an atmosphere that is both enchanting and timeless. As the sun dips below the horizon, casting a warm glow over the village and the sea, visitors find themselves captivated by a sense of tranquility and wonder. Eze is more than a destination; it's a journey through time and emotion, an exploration of the connection between humanity and the breathtaking landscapes that inspire us.

From wandering through the narrow alleys to contemplating the sea from the Jardin Exotique's heights, Eze invites visitors to slow down, to embrace the moment, and to carry the memory of its beauty long after they depart. In the embrace of Eze's ancient walls and panoramic vistas, travelers find a sanctuary that transcends the ordinary, leaving an indelible imprint on the heart and soul.

Gastronomy and Cuisine:

When exploring the enchanting landscapes and rich culture of the French Riviera, your journey is incomplete without indulging in its exquisite culinary offerings. The flavors of the region are a reflection of its coastal bounty, Mediterranean influences, and historical significance. Here are some local specialties that will tantalize your taste buds:

Nicoise Salad: A Symphony of Freshness and Flavor
Originating in the city of Nice, the Nicoise salad is a masterpiece of simplicity and vibrant ingredients. A true embodiment of the Mediterranean diet, this salad features a colorful array of fresh vegetables, olives, and anchovies, all drizzled with olive oil and often adorned with a boiled egg. The crispness of lettuce, the sweetness of ripe tomatoes, the brininess of olives, and the umami punch of anchovies come together in a harmonious blend that captures the essence of the Riviera's coastal abundance.

Bouillabaisse: A Hearty Taste of Maritime Heritage

Bouillabaisse is more than just a fish stew; it's a celebration of the sea that has sustained the region for centuries. This flavorful dish is a testament to the Mediterranean's rich maritime history. Typically made with a variety of fresh fish and shellfish, cooked together with aromatic herbs, tomatoes, and a hint of saffron, bouillabaisse creates a symphony of fragrances and tastes. Served with a side of rouille—a garlicky mayonnaise-like sauce—and crusty bread, this dish beckons you to savor each spoonful while basking in the coastal ambiance.

Socca: A Culinary Treasure from the Streets

As you wander through the bustling streets and markets of the French Riviera, you'll likely encounter the delightful aroma of socca wafting from street stalls. Socca is a traditional street food favorite made from a simple batter of chickpea flour, water, and olive oil. Cooked on a large griddle until crisp and slightly charred, this savory pancake offers a satisfying blend of nutty flavors and tender textures. Often sprinkled with a touch of black pepper, socca is best enjoyed straight from the griddle, served in slices for a quick and delectable snack.

Ratatouille: A Tapestry of Mediterranean Vegetables

Ratatouille is a vegetable medley that embodies the essence of Provençal cuisine. This hearty and flavorful dish combines a variety of seasonal vegetables such as eggplant, zucchini, bell peppers, and tomatoes, stewed with aromatic herbs like thyme and rosemary. The result is a harmonious blend of textures and flavors that showcases the region's agricultural richness.

Pissaladière: A Provençal Twist on Pizza

Pissaladière is a Provencal specialty that draws its inspiration from pizza but has its own unique character. A thin dough base is topped with caramelized onions, black olives, and anchovies, often seasoned with herbs like thyme or oregano. This savory treat is a testament to the Mediterranean's affinity for bold flavors and simple yet satisfying combinations.

Salade Niçoise: A Culinary Ode to the Sea
Similar to the Nicoise Salad, the Salade Niçoise pays homage to the coastal bounty of the French Riviera. Featuring tuna, hard-boiled eggs, green beans, and potatoes, this salad is a hearty and wholesome meal. Anchovies, olives, and a drizzle of olive oil provide the perfect finishing touch to this refreshing dish.

Tarte Tropezienne: A Sweet Indulgence from Saint-Tropez
For those with a sweet tooth, the Tarte Tropezienne is a dessert that's hard to resist. Originating in Saint-Tropez, this delicate pastry comprises a brioche-like dough filled with a luscious cream made from a blend of whipped cream and pastry cream. The top is often sprinkled with pearl sugar, giving it a delightful crunch that contrasts with the pillowy softness within.

Mediterranean Seafood Platter: A Feast of the Ocean's Finest
While not a specific dish, a Mediterranean seafood platter is a must-try experience when visiting the Riviera. Indulge in an array of freshly caught seafood, from succulent prawns and mussels to tender calamari and octopus. Grilled, fried, or simply prepared with a touch of lemon and olive oil, the seafood platter showcases the region's deep connection to the sea and its culinary prowess.

Local Tips:

Take a scenic drive along the "Corniche" roads for breathtaking coastal views:

The Corniche roads are a network of picturesque routes that wind along the cliffs and coastline of the French Riviera. Each Corniche offers a unique perspective of the Mediterranean Sea, with stunning vistas and panoramic overlooks at every turn. Consider driving along the Grande Corniche for sweeping views of the coastline and the Mediterranean beyond. The Moyenne Corniche offers a balance between scenic beauty and easy access to charming towns, while the Basse Corniche takes you closer to the water's edge, revealing hidden coves and beaches. Along these routes, you'll encounter charming villages, historic sites, and ample opportunities to stop and capture the breathtaking scenery.

Visit during the shoulder seasons (spring and fall) for pleasant weather and fewer crowds:

The French Riviera experiences a Mediterranean climate, which means mild winters and hot summers. To make the most of your visit, consider planning your trip during the shoulder seasons of spring (April to June) and fall (September to October). During these months, the weather is generally pleasant, with comfortable temperatures and a lower chance of rain. Additionally, you'll avoid the peak tourist crowds that descend upon the region during the summer months. This allows for a more relaxed and immersive experience as you explore the attractions, dine in local eateries, and enjoy the beaches without the hustle and bustle.

Explore local markets for artisanal products and fresh produce:

One of the joys of traveling through the French Riviera is experiencing the local flavors and products that define the region. Take time to explore the vibrant markets that dot the towns and villages along the coast. These markets offer a treasure trove of artisanal products, fresh produce, and unique crafts. Engage with friendly vendors as you sample ripe fruits, local cheeses, and aromatic spices. Wander through stalls filled with colorful Provençal textiles, handmade ceramics, and fragrant flowers. Notable markets include the Cours Saleya in Nice, the Forville Market in Cannes, and the Ventimiglia Market just across the border in Italy. Exploring these markets not only lets you connect with the local culture but also provides an opportunity to bring a piece of the Mediterranean lifestyle home with you.

The French Riviera offers a blend of cultural exploration, seaside relaxation, and upscale living. Its charm has inspired artists, writers, and travelers for centuries, and its allure continues to captivate visitors from around the world.

Cinque Terre's Colorful Charms

Nestled along the rugged Ligurian coastline of Italy, Cinque Terre stands as a mesmerizing testament to the harmonious coexistence of nature and human architecture. The name "Cinque Terre" translates to "Five Lands," and it refers to the five charming villages that make up this UNESCO World Heritage Site: Monterosso al Mare, Vernazza, Corniglia, Manarola, and Riomaggiore.

The Enchanting Villages

Cinque Terre, a collection of five exquisite villages nestled along the rugged Ligurian coastline of Italy, presents an unparalleled display of diversity within unity. While they each have their distinct personalities, these villages—Monterosso al Mare, Vernazza, Corniglia, Manarola, and Riomaggiore—share a common bond of picturesque beauty that weaves together their stories, capturing the hearts of all who visit.

A Clifftop Tapestry

As you approach each village, a sense of awe envelops you. The buildings appear to defy gravity, nestled precariously on the cliffs that plunge dramatically into the crystalline waters of the Ligurian Sea. This architecture, an ingenious adaptation to the challenging terrain, creates an otherworldly scene that feels both harmonious and daring. The sheer proximity of the buildings to the sea fosters an intimate connection between the land and the water, as if nature and human creation are engaged in a timeless dance.

Hues of Nature and Imagination

Perhaps the most enchanting feature of these villages is the kaleidoscope of colors that grace their facades. Pastel hues of orange, pink, and yellow are carefully chosen to harmonize with the natural beauty of the surroundings. It's as if the villagers collaborated with the sea and sky to create a harmonious symphony of shades that delights the eyes and nourishes the soul. The vibrancy of these colors is particularly pronounced against the cerulean backdrop of the Mediterranean, forming a breathtaking visual contrast that ignites a sense of wonder.

Monterosso al Mare: The Graceful Giant

Monterosso al Mare, the largest of the five villages, exudes a sense of openness and space. Its expansive beachfront, dotted with colorful umbrellas, invites visitors to relax and soak up the sun's warmth. Here, the vivid colors of the buildings blend seamlessly with the verdant hills that envelop the village, creating a tranquil haven that contrasts with the exuberant energy of the sea.

Vernazza: The Jewel of the Coast

Vernazza, often described as the crown jewel of Cinque Terre, captures hearts with its timeless beauty. The village's small harbor is a haven for fishing boats, and the gentle waves serenade visitors as they explore the narrow streets and hidden corners. The vibrant facades of Vernazza's buildings harmonize with the village's lively spirit, as locals and travelers mingle in charming piazzas, sharing stories and laughter.

Corniglia: A Tranquil Perch

Perched atop a rocky promontory, Corniglia offers a different perspective of Cinque Terre. To reach this village, one must ascend a flight of steps, providing a sense of seclusion that's rewarded with sweeping panoramic views. The buildings' warm colors, combined with the terraced vineyards that surround the village, create an idyllic setting that evokes a feeling of timelessness.

Manarola: The Romantic Hideaway

Manarola, perhaps the most romantic of the villages, enchants with its intimate charm. The village is famous for its enchanting tunnel of love, a pathway adorned with vibrant bougainvillaeas that leads to a rocky shore perfect for watching sunsets. The pastel buildings seem to embrace visitors, inviting them to explore hidden alleys and relish the simple joys of life.

Riomaggiore: Where Tradition Meets Modernity

Riomaggiore, the southernmost village, is a testament to the blending of tradition and modernity. Its colorful buildings climb up the hillside, and the harbor bustles with life as fishermen bring in their catches. The village's vibrant energy is juxtaposed with the serenity of its surroundings, offering a glimpse into the harmonious coexistence of the past and the present.

A Tapestry Woven with Stories

In each village's unique character and vibrant colors, one discovers not only a feast for the eyes but also a glimpse into the lives of the people who call Cinque Terre home. The pastel facades tell stories of generations who have thrived in this remarkable landscape, adapting to its challenges and celebrating its gifts. The azure backdrop of the Mediterranean serves as a canvas upon which the villagers have painted their hopes, dreams, and resilience.

Cinque Terre's villages, each an individual stroke in a masterpiece of human creativity and nature's grandeur, beckon travelers to immerse themselves in a world where time seems to stand still. They embody the essence of the Mediterranean's allure—its vibrant colors, rich history, and the profound connection between land and sea. The picturesque beauty that unites these villages captures the heart and ignites the imagination, inviting all who visit to become a part of Cinque Terre's ongoing story.

Coastal Trails and Terraced Vineyards

The network of scenic hiking trails that gracefully weaves through Cinque Terre is nothing short of a hiker's paradise. Among these trails, the crown jewel is undeniably the Sentiero Azzurro, aptly named the "Blue Trail," which serves as a poetic conduit between the five picturesque villages. This trail is more than a path; it's a passage through time, offering an intimate connection with the land, the sea, and the stories of those who have called Cinque Terre home for centuries.

The Sentiero Azzurro: A Path of Wonder

The Sentiero Azzurro is not merely a means of traversing the villages – it's a sensory voyage, an immersion into the heart of Cinque Terre's natural and cultural tapestry. The trail winds along the cliffs, offering a ballet of breathtaking vistas that encompass the boundless azure sea, the quaint villages nestled on rocky outcrops, and the lush terraced hillsides that characterize the landscape. Each step along the path is a new revelation, a fresh perspective that unveils the nuances of this coastal haven.

Panoramic Poetry: Views to Enchant the Soul

Hiking along the Sentiero Azzurro is like entering a gallery of panoramic artistry. From vantage points strategically placed along the trail, the beholder is rewarded with sweeping views that seem almost surreal in their beauty. As you stand on these lookout points, the world below transforms into a mesmerizing mosaic – cerulean waves lapping against the rugged shoreline, the colorful village houses cascading down the cliffs, and the expanse of the horizon extending as far as the eye can see. These vistas not only capture the magnificence of nature but also offer a glimpse into the lives of the fishermen, farmers, and artisans who have thrived in this region for generations.

A Stroll Through the Vineyards: Tasting the Terroir

As the Sentiero Azzurro leads you through its enchanting landscapes, it also unveils the deeply rooted relationship between the people of Cinque Terre and their land. One of the most captivating aspects of this trail is its passage through the terraced vineyards that cling to the steep hillsides. These meticulously cultivated vineyards have been a labor of love for generations of farmers who recognized the potential of this rugged terrain to produce exceptional wines.

Walking through these vineyards is a sensory symphony – the earthy aroma of the soil, the rustling of leaves in the sea breeze, and the sun's warm embrace combine to create an experience that's as much about the senses as it is about the scenery. The terraces themselves are a testament to human ingenuity, as they transform challenging topography into arable land that nurtures grapes, yielding wines that reflect the essence of the region. The trek is not only a visual feast but a connection to the livelihoods, traditions, and flavors that have been cultivated here for centuries.

Preserving Beauty: Walking with Responsibility

As you embark on your journey along the Sentiero Azzurro, it's vital to remember that you're treading upon hallowed ground. Cinque Terre's beauty is fragile, and its sustainability relies on the efforts of both locals and visitors. Responsible hiking practices are essential to protect the trails, flora, and fauna that contribute to the region's charm.

Respect for the environment and the local culture means staying on designated paths, avoiding disrupting wildlife, and adhering to any trail regulations. Supporting the Cinque Terre National Park's initiatives for sustainable tourism ensures that generations to come will have the privilege of experiencing the same untouched beauty that you encounter on your journey.

The Sentiero Azzurro's Endless Gifts

As you step along the Sentiero Azzurro, you're not just hiking a trail – you're writing your own chapter in the story of Cinque Terre. Each twist and turn is an invitation to explore, reflect, and connect with the natural world and the human history that has unfolded in this coastal haven. The Sentiero Azzurro is more than a path; it's a bridge between past and present, a canvas of breathtaking vistas, and an embodiment of the spirit of Cinque Terre – a spirit that continues to inspire and captivate all who walk its trails.

Local Cuisine and Seafood Delights

The culinary scene of Cinque Terre is a true testament to the region's deep connection with the sea and its bounties. As you wander through the picturesque villages perched on the cliffs overlooking the azure waters of the Ligurian Sea, you'll find that the local cuisine is not just a meal but a journey into the heart of Mediterranean flavors and traditions.

A Symphony of Seafood

Seafood reigns supreme in Cinque Terre, and it's easy to understand why. With the Mediterranean right at its doorstep, the villages have long embraced a fishing tradition that has shaped their way of life and culinary heritage. Locals have perfected the art of transforming the day's catch into exquisite dishes that showcase the freshest flavors of the sea.

Trofie al Pesto: A Basil-Infused Delight

Among the signature dishes of Cinque Terre is "trofie al pesto," a pasta dish that encapsulates the essence of Ligurian cuisine. Trofie, a short, twisted pasta, is the perfect canvas for the region's renowned pesto sauce. This sauce is a vibrant combination of fresh basil leaves, pine nuts, garlic, Parmesan cheese, and extra-virgin olive oil, all ground together to create a fragrant and verdant masterpiece.

Every bite of trofie al pesto is a celebration of the land's bounty, with the aroma of basil transporting you to sun-soaked gardens. The dish's simplicity highlights the harmony of its ingredients and the meticulous care that goes into crafting a sauce that's both rich and delicate.

Frittura di Pesce: A Seaside Symphony

Another culinary gem that exemplifies Cinque Terre's connection to the sea is "frittura di pesce." This dish offers a tantalizing array of lightly fried seafood, allowing the natural flavors to shine through. A platter of frittura di pesce is a feast for the senses, with crispy and tender morsels of squid, shrimp, anchovies, and other treasures of the sea.

As you indulge in this delightful medley, you can almost taste the salty sea breeze and feel the warmth of the sun on your skin. It's a dish that encapsulates the carefree spirit of coastal living and invites you to revel in the simple pleasures of life by the water.

Celebrating Terroir and Tradition

The culinary treasures of Cinque Terre go beyond these iconic dishes, encompassing a wide range of flavors that celebrate both the land and the sea. Ligurian olive oil, known for its delicate and fruity notes, plays a central role in many dishes, enhancing everything from pasta to seafood.

Cinque Terre is also famous for its wines, particularly the white wine varieties that thrive in its unique microclimate. Sipping a glass of Sciacchetrà, a sweet and aromatic dessert wine, is like savoring the very essence of the region's sun-soaked hillsides.

A Local Experience

One of the most remarkable aspects of enjoying Cinque Terre's culinary scene is the chance to engage with the locals and their way of life. You'll find quaint trattorias and osterias tucked away in the alleys, where the ambiance is as inviting as the food itself. Engaging in conversation with the proprietors, who often source their ingredients from nearby markets and fishermen, adds a layer of authenticity to the experience.

Savoring Memories

As you savor each bite of trofie al pesto or sample the delights of frittura di pesce, you're not just enjoying a meal – you're creating memories that will forever be associated with the flavors of Cinque Terre. The cuisine is a reflection of the region's rich history, its relationship with the Mediterranean, and the passionate dedication of its people to preserving their heritage.

So, as you explore the colorful villages and breathtaking landscapes of Cinque Terre, make sure to set aside time to immerse yourself in its culinary delights. From the first taste to the last lingering note, the journey through Mediterranean flavors will be a highlight of your visit, a sensory exploration of a place where the land and sea intertwine on every plate.

Artisan Craftsmanship

Wandering through the enchanting cobblestone streets and meandering narrow alleyways of Cinque Terre is akin to stepping into a living canvas where craftsmanship and heritage come together in a harmonious dance. These pathways, worn smooth by generations of footsteps, lead not just to breathtaking vistas but also to a world of artisanal wonders that tell the tales of this coastal paradise. From intricately adorned ceramics to handwoven textiles reflecting the hues of the sea, each piece carries a fragment of Cinque Terre's essence, inviting you to embrace its spirit long after your visit.

The Artisanal Journey

As you stroll through the charming villages of Cinque Terre, you'll find hidden gems nestled between pastel-hued facades. Artisan workshops, some hidden in the nooks and crannies of centuries-old buildings, emanate the hum of creativity. These workshops serve as sanctuaries where skilled artisans meticulously hone their crafts, passing down techniques and traditions through the ages.

Ceramics that Whisper of the Sea

Cinque Terre's connection to the Mediterranean is beautifully encapsulated in its ceramic creations. Local artisans skillfully mold clay into intricate forms, embellishing them with vibrant designs that mirror the colors of the sea and the villages themselves. Ceramics bearing images of boats gently swaying in azure waters, blooming flowers against sun-kissed walls, and picturesque landscapes of the coastline awaken a sense of nostalgia for the moments spent here.

Textiles Woven with Coastal Dreams

The rhythm of the sea finds its echo in the handwoven textiles that grace the workshops of Cinque Terre. Delicate fabrics adorned with patterns reminiscent of ocean waves and coastal flora transport you to the tranquil shores with every touch. Skilled hands deftly manipulate threads, conjuring images of fishing nets and salty breezes that infuse each piece with the coastal mystique.

Capturing the Spirit of Cinque Terre

Bringing a piece of Cinque Terre home with you goes beyond owning an item; it's about encapsulating the memories, emotions, and experiences you've gathered during your journey. The ceramics that once adorned a quaint shop window become the vessels of your memories, evoking the laughter shared with friends over a meal by the sea. The textiles you carefully select tell stories of the vibrant sunsets that painted the sky as you explored the villages.

A Legacy of Craftsmanship

The artistry of Cinque Terre is not merely a commercial endeavor; it's a living testament to the dedication and passion of the local artisans. Many of these workshops have been in families for generations, handed down from parents to children. Each piece crafted is a labor of love, a bridge between past and present that celebrates the rich history of this coastal enclave.

Supporting Local Traditions

By indulging in these artisanal treasures, you become part of a greater story. Your appreciation for the crafts sustains the continuation of these traditions, ensuring that the generations to come can also experience the magic of handcrafted goods that hold the very soul of Cinque Terre. Through your support, these artisans can continue to breathe life into their creations and inspire others to explore their own creative journeys.

A Lasting Connection

Every time you gaze at a ceramic plate adorned with coastal scenes or wrap yourself in a handwoven textile, you'll be transported back to Cinque Terre's labyrinthine streets, the aroma of the sea, and the warm embrace of its people. The artistry you bring home isn't just a souvenir; it's a portal through which you can relive your journey, share its tales with others, and be reminded of the beauty that lies within the human touch.

In Cinque Terre, art is not a mere luxury; it's a way of life. It's a celebration of the land's natural beauty, a reflection of its vibrant culture, and an embodiment of the enduring spirit of the people. These artisanal creations, woven with love and steeped in history, are a tribute to the magic of this coastal haven – an everlasting reminder that even in the modern world, the heartbeat of tradition and creativity still pulses strong.

Sustainable Tourism and Preservation Efforts

Nestled within the embrace of the Ligurian coastline, Cinque Terre stands not only as a testament to the artistry of human architecture but also as a living embodiment of nature's wonders. Recognized as a UNESCO World Heritage Site and a protected national park, the region has made it a paramount mission to safeguard its natural beauty and cultural heritage for future generations. At the heart of this endeavor lies a commitment to sustainable tourism, a delicate balance between sharing the marvels of the region and ensuring its preservation.

Safeguarding a Precious Ecosystem

Cinque Terre's unique geography, characterized by its terraced landscapes, rich biodiversity, and pristine shoreline, demands careful stewardship. With a mosaic of habitats that range from steep cliffs to rocky shores and lush vineyards, the area hosts a myriad of plant and animal species that contribute to its ecological tapestry. This intricately woven ecosystem, however, is vulnerable to the impacts of unrestricted tourism.

To counteract these threats, local authorities, in collaboration with national agencies and environmental organizations, have implemented a series of measures to maintain the ecological equilibrium. These include designated walking paths to prevent soil erosion, restrictions on unauthorized fishing, and proactive reforestation efforts. By weaving the fabric of human exploration into the fabric of nature's design, Cinque Terre endeavors to create an environment where the footprints of visitors leave nothing but memories.

Balancing Visitor Numbers

The charm of Cinque Terre's villages, with their pastel-hued homes clinging to cliffsides and the azure waters of the Ligurian Sea lapping at their feet, has captivated the imagination of travelers from around the globe. However, with popularity comes the challenge of managing the influx of visitors in a way that preserves the region's authenticity. The local communities, in collaboration with tourism authorities, have taken proactive steps to address this issue.

By implementing a system that controls the number of visitors allowed at any given time, Cinque Terre has achieved a harmonious balance between welcoming tourists and maintaining the tranquility of the villages. This approach not only enhances the experience for visitors by providing a more intimate encounter with the surroundings but also safeguards the quality of life for the locals who call Cinque Terre home.

Cultural Heritage: A Treasure to Be Cherished

Beyond its natural allure, Cinque Terre is also steeped in a rich cultural tapestry. The villages' architecture, traditions, and way of life have evolved over centuries, shaped by the rhythms of the sea and the spirit of the land. Recognizing the importance of preserving this intangible heritage, the region has engaged in efforts to foster a deep appreciation for local customs among both residents and visitors.

Educational programs, guided tours, and interactive experiences allow travelers to engage with the culture of Cinque Terre in meaningful ways. Whether it's participating in traditional grape harvests or learning the art of Ligurian cuisine, these initiatives create connections that transcend the superficial and forge a deeper bond between people and place. In turn, this cultural exchange encourages respect for the past and a commitment to its continuation.

Empowering a Sustainable Legacy

As the tides of tourism ebb and flow, Cinque Terre remains steadfast in its commitment to sustainability. Its story is not merely one of picturesque villages and breathtaking vistas; it is a narrative of resilience, of a community that has united to protect the treasures that define it. By championing sustainable practices, Cinque Terre serves as a beacon of hope and inspiration for destinations around the world grappling with the challenges of tourism's impact.

In an era where the global travel landscape is evolving, Cinque Terre stands as a model of how responsible stewardship and mindful exploration can coexist in perfect harmony. With every step taken on its scenic trails, every shared moment with locals, and every heartfelt connection forged, visitors become custodians of this precious corner of the world. Cinque Terre's legacy of sustainable tourism is a testament to the power of shared responsibility and a reminder that, through our choices, we can ensure that the wonders of today remain the treasures of tomorrow.

Capturing the Essence

Cinque Terre's allure goes beyond the breathtaking landscapes and picturesque villages that greet your eyes. It's a place where time seems to slow down, inviting you to embrace a different rhythm of life—one that is intimately connected to its history, its people, and the profound experiences it offers.

The Warm Hospitality of Locals

One of the most captivating aspects of Cinque Terre is the genuine warmth of its locals. As you wander through the labyrinthine streets and alleyways, you'll find yourself greeted with smiles and open arms. The villagers have mastered the art of making visitors feel like cherished guests, imparting a sense of belonging that transforms your stay into a personal journey.

Engaging in conversations with the locals can reveal a wealth of knowledge about the area's traditions, stories, and the evolution of their way of life. Whether you're sharing stories with fishermen who have cast their nets in the same waters for generations or engaging in lively discussions with artisans who infuse their craft with the spirit of Cinque Terre, these encounters add a layer of authenticity to your experience.

The Art of Savoring Life's Simple Pleasures

In Cinque Terre, the concept of dolce far niente, or the sweetness of doing nothing, becomes an art form. As you meander through the villages, you'll notice that the pace of life here is intentionally unhurried. Locals and visitors alike embrace the simple joys—a leisurely stroll along the harbor, a pause to admire the sunset, or a moment to relish the flavors of a gelato by the sea.

This art of savoring life's pleasures isn't just about indulgence; it's a celebration of the present moment. It's an invitation to detach from the demands of modern life and immerse yourself in the beauty of the surroundings. In Cinque Terre, you'll discover that the most profound experiences often arise from the simplest of moments.

A Journey Through Time and Tradition

Cinque Terre is a living testament to the resilience of communities deeply rooted in their traditions. The villages have weathered the challenges of time, from pirate raids to landslides, and have emerged stronger, their stories woven into the very fabric of the region.

Every stone, every alley, and every square holds a story waiting to be discovered. The ancient watchtowers that once stood guard against maritime threats now stand as silent sentinels overlooking the sea. The terraced vineyards, painstakingly crafted over centuries, pay homage to the industriousness and perseverance of generations past.

As you explore these five lands, you'll come across remnants of a past that continues to shape the present. Each village has its own history, its own triumphs and tribulations, and as you listen to the tales shared by locals, you'll gain a deeper appreciation for the resilience and spirit of the people who call this rugged coast home.

Crafting Timeless Memories

Cinque Terre has a magical way of etching itself into your memory. It's not just about the stunning photographs you'll capture—though those will undoubtedly be cherished mementos—it's about the intangible moments that become an intrinsic part of who you are.

Whether it's the sound of waves crashing against the cliffs as you watch the sunrise, the laughter shared with newfound friends while sipping wine on a terrace, or the feeling of community as you join locals in a traditional celebration, these experiences become imprinted on your heart.

Long after you've left Cinque Terre, the scent of the sea breeze, the taste of fresh seafood, and the echoes of laughter in the village squares will transport you back to this enchanting corner of the Mediterranean. The stories you've heard, the connections you've made, and the memories you've created will endure, a timeless treasure that you can revisit whenever you close your eyes and let your mind wander back to the colorful charms of Cinque Terre.

Tips for Exploring Cinque Terre:

1. Plan Your Hiking Adventure:

- Research the different hiking trails available in Cinque Terre and choose the one that suits your fitness level and interests.
- Check the trail conditions and weather forecasts before embarking on your hike, as some paths might be closed due to maintenance or adverse weather conditions.
- Pack comfortable hiking shoes, a hat, sunglasses, sunscreen, and plenty of water to stay hydrated during your hike.

2. Savor the Local Wines:

- Cinque Terre is known for its unique wine, Sciacchetrà, a sweet and aromatic white wine made from locally grown grapes.
- Take the opportunity to visit local wineries and vineyards, where you can participate in wine tastings and learn about the winemaking process.
- Pair your wine with regional specialties like focaccia, local cheeses, and freshly caught seafood for an authentic culinary experience.

3. Soak in the Vineyard Views:

- The terraced vineyards that cling to the cliffs offer not only a source of excellent wine but also stunning panoramic views of the sea and villages.
- Consider taking breaks during your hike to sit on a vineyard terrace, enjoy a picnic, and bask in the beauty of your surroundings.
- Capture the breathtaking landscapes through your camera lens to preserve the memories of this unique experience.

4. Practice Responsible Tourism:

- Stick to the designated hiking trails to protect the fragile ecosystem and prevent erosion of the cliffs.
- Respect the local flora and fauna by not disturbing plants or animals and disposing of trash properly.
- Engage with the local community by interacting respectfully with residents and adhering to their customs and traditions.

5. Support Sustainable Tourism:

- Consider staying in locally owned accommodations, such as bed and breakfasts or family-run guesthouses, to contribute directly to the community.
- Purchase souvenirs and goods from local artisans and businesses, supporting the local economy and preserving the authenticity of the region.
- Educate yourself about the conservation efforts in place and donate to organizations working towards the preservation of Cinque Terre's natural beauty.

6. Embrace the Slow Pace:

- Cinque Terre is a place to unwind and appreciate the simple pleasures of life. Take your time to savor the beauty around you, whether you're hiking, dining, or simply enjoying the coastal views.
- Immerse yourself in the local lifestyle by striking up conversations with locals, learning about their traditions, and participating in cultural events if possible.

Remember, Cinque Terre's charm lies not only in its stunning landscapes but also in the meaningful connections you make with the environment and the people. By following these tips, you can ensure that your exploration of this remarkable region leaves a positive impact while creating memories to cherish.

Ancient Marvels in Greece and Turkey

Roaming through Athens: Where History Comes Alive

Athens, the capital of Greece, stands as a living testament to the cradle of Western civilization. With its rich history and iconic landmarks, this ancient city offers travelers a unique opportunity to step back in time and immerse themselves in the stories of antiquity.

Acropolis: A Glimpse into the Past

The Acropolis of Athens stands as a majestic time capsule, preserving the rich history and architectural achievements of ancient Greece. Perched on a rocky hill overlooking the city, this elevated citadel is an iconic symbol of Athens and a UNESCO World Heritage Site. As you approach the Acropolis, its grandeur becomes increasingly apparent, drawing you into a world where gods and mortals once converged.

The Magnificent Parthenon
At the pinnacle of the Acropolis, the Parthenon reigns supreme. This temple, dedicated to the goddess Athena, represents a triumph of architecture and engineering. Its impressive facade boasts a series of majestic Doric columns, meticulously carved with fluted details and elegant proportions. The Parthenon's pediments and friezes depict scenes from Greek mythology, reflecting the profound influence of storytelling on art and culture.

Awakening Awe and Reverence
Ascending the marble steps of the Acropolis, you step into an environment that resonates with an aura of reverence. The Temples of Erechtheion and Athena Nike flank the Parthenon, each with its unique design and purpose. The Erechtheion's six Caryatid columns, sculpted in the form of draped female figures, evoke a sense of graceful strength. The Temple of Athena Nike, dedicated to the goddess of victory, features delicate friezes and an elegant Ionic design

that speaks to the Athenians' appreciation for artistic nuance.

The Golden Age of Athens
The Acropolis is a living tribute to the Golden Age of Athens, a period of unprecedented cultural and intellectual achievement during the 5th century BC. This era gave rise to philosophers like Socrates, Plato, and Aristotle, whose ideas continue to shape modern thought. As you stand amidst the ruins of the Acropolis, you are transported back to a time when democracy flourished, and the pursuit of knowledge was held in the highest esteem.

The Parthenon: A Triumph of Architecture

The Parthenon stands as a cornerstone of ancient Greek architecture, a true testament to the mastery of design, precision, and aesthetics. Dedicated to Athena Parthenos, the city's patron goddess, the Parthenon's construction was led by the renowned architect Phidias and funded by the spoils of the Greco-Persian Wars. Beyond its stunning visual impact, the Parthenon carries profound symbolism and historical significance that resonate through the ages.

Doric Splendor
The Parthenon exemplifies the Doric order, an architectural style characterized by sturdy, fluted columns supporting an entablature of alternating triglyphs and metopes. These columns were engineered with a slight curvature to create an optical illusion of straight lines, compensating for the visual distortion caused by human perception. The harmony and precision of the Doric elements contribute to the temple's sublime beauty.

The Pediments and Friezes

The Parthenon's pediments and friezes are veritable masterpieces of sculptural artistry. The eastern pediment depicts the birth of Athena, emerging fully grown from the head of her father Zeus. The western pediment narrates the contest between Athena and Poseidon for the patronage of Athens. The continuous frieze encircling the inner chamber, known as the cella, portrays the Panathenaic Procession, an elaborate festival honoring Athena. These sculptures not only showcase the Greeks' skill in stone carving but also their commitment to storytelling through art.

Human Achievement and Divine Grandeur
As you stand before the Parthenon, it's hard not to be overwhelmed by a sense of awe and admiration. The temple's grandeur reflects not only the Greeks' reverence for their gods but also their belief in the potential of human achievement. The intricate carvings, meticulously designed proportions, and architectural innovations embody the ideals of balance, harmony, and rationality that characterized the Golden Age of Athens.

Legacy and Inspiration
The Parthenon's influence extends far beyond its physical presence. Its architectural principles have informed countless buildings and structures throughout history, from neoclassical designs to government buildings in democratic societies. Its enduring legacy serves as a reminder of the indomitable human spirit and the ability to create enduring works of art and architecture that transcend time and culture.

Agora: The Heart of Civic Life

Descending from the Acropolis, you'll find yourself stepping into the ancient Agora of Athens, a sprawling open space that was once the bustling heart of civic and social activity. In the shadow of the Parthenon's grandeur, the Agora played a pivotal role in shaping the cultural and political landscape of ancient Athens. Here, Socrates philosophized, politicians debated, and the foundations of democracy were laid.

Economic Exchange and Social Interaction
The Agora was not only a marketplace for goods but also a vibrant hub for intellectual discourse, political engagement, and social interaction. Traders and merchants from various corners of the ancient world converged here to exchange goods, cultures, and ideas. The market's stalls were filled with pottery, textiles, spices, and other commodities, creating a colorful tapestry of diversity.

Socrates and Philosophical Dialogue
One of the most iconic figures associated with the Agora is the philosopher Socrates. He often engaged in philosophical debates and discussions with fellow Athenians, challenging conventional wisdom and encouraging critical thinking. Socrates' famous Socratic method, a form of dialectical questioning, sought to elicit deeper insights by dismantling surface-level assumptions.

Birthplace of Democracy
The Agora's significance in the birth of democracy cannot be overstated. It was in this space that citizens of Athens gathered to participate in the democratic process, casting their votes on important matters. The term "agora" itself signifies not only a physical space but also a concept of democratic citizenship and participation. The Athenian democracy that emerged from this civic arena laid the foundation for modern governance and the ideals of citizen empowerment.

Temple of Hephaestus: Architectural Marvel

Adjacent to the Agora stands the Temple of Hephaestus, a remarkably well-preserved Doric temple dedicated to the god of craftsmanship and blacksmiths. This temple showcases the mastery of ancient Greek architecture, with its orderly columns and intricate friezes depicting scenes from Greek mythology. As you walk through its porticoes and explore its chambers, you're transported to a time when craftsmanship was celebrated as an art form.

National Archaeological Museum: Treasures Preserved

For those seeking a deeper connection to Athens' rich past, the National Archaeological Museum stands as a repository of antiquities that span millennia. This museum, one of the world's most important archaeological collections, offers a journey through time, allowing visitors to witness the evolution of Greek art, culture, and civilization.

Artifacts that Tell Stories
The museum's halls are filled with an astonishing array of artifacts, each telling a unique story of Greece's past. Intricately designed pottery decorated with scenes of mythology and daily life provide insights into ancient aesthetics. Statues of gods, warriors, and philosophers evoke a sense of the divine and human aspirations that shaped the Greek psyche.

Mask of Agamemnon
One of the museum's most famous exhibits is the Mask of Agamemnon, a stunning gold death mask discovered in the legendary archaeological site of Mycenae. This artifact, associated with the Mycenaean civilization of the Bronze Age, captures the mystique and opulence of ancient rulers. Its craftsmanship and symbolic significance provide a glimpse into the rituals and beliefs of a bygone era.

Bronze Statue of Poseidon
Another remarkable highlight is the bronze statue of Poseidon, often referred to as the "Poseidon of Artemision." This awe-inspiring sculpture showcases the mastery of Greek sculptors in rendering the human form and capturing the essence of mythological figures. The dynamic pose and intricate details of the statue create a sense of movement and vitality, embodying the spirit of the sea god.

Plaka: A Glimpse of Old Athens

Wandering through the charming streets of Plaka, you'll experience a delightful juxtaposition of old and new, a testament to Athens' enduring spirit and evolving identity. This historic neighborhood, nestled at the foot of the Acropolis, is a treasure trove of neoclassical architecture, cobblestone alleys, and vibrant bougainvillaea.

Neoclassical Elegance
Plaka's architecture is a blend of styles that reflects the city's diverse history. Neoclassical buildings adorned with ornate balconies and wrought-iron railings stand alongside Ottoman-era structures with their distinct wooden features. This fusion of influences creates a visual narrative of the neighborhood's evolution over time.

Charming Alleys and Local Flavors
As you stroll through Plaka's labyrinthine alleys, you'll discover a plethora of small shops, art galleries, and traditional tavernas. The inviting aromas of Greek cuisine waft through the air, inviting you to savor local specialties such as moussaka, souvlaki, and spanakopita. Seating in the tavernas spills out onto the cobblestone streets, creating a convivial atmosphere that encourages relaxation and connection.

An Escape from Modernity

Plaka offers a reprieve from the bustling modernity of the city, allowing visitors to step back in time and experience Athens through a different lens. The ambiance is both nostalgic and vibrant, a reminder of the city's rich history while also celebrating its contemporary creative energy. Amidst the narrow streets and charming squares, Plaka invites you to slow down, immerse yourself in the local culture, and relish the unique character of this timeless neighborhood.

Theatre of Dionysus: Drama Unveiled

Perched on the southern slopes of the Acropolis, the Theatre of Dionysus stands as a testament to Athens' profound contributions to theater and drama. This ancient amphitheater, named after the Greek god of wine and fertility, is where the works of some of history's greatest playwrights were first performed, leaving an indelible mark on the world of storytelling.

Birthplace of Tragedy and Comedy

The Theatre of Dionysus was the primary venue for the Athenian dramatic festivals, where playwrights competed for recognition and acclaim. It was here that the works of Aeschylus, Sophocles, Euripides, and Aristophanes were brought to life, sparking the birth of tragedy and comedy. The ancient Greeks' affinity for theater was a reflection of their deep engagement with both the human and divine aspects of life.

Architectural Marvel

The amphitheater itself is an architectural marvel, hewn into the natural landscape to accommodate thousands of spectators. Rows of stone seats cascade down the hillside, culminating in an orchestra pit and a raised stage. The seating arrangement reflected the hierarchy of Athenian society, with the most privileged spectators occupying the front rows.

Whispers of the Past
Standing amidst the worn stone seats of the Theatre of Dionysus, you can almost hear the echoes of ancient performances. Imagine the audience's anticipation as they awaited the unfolding drama, the actors' emotive voices resonating through the open air, and the collective reactions of laughter, tears, and contemplation. This amphitheater serves as a bridge connecting the contemporary theatergoer to the earliest roots of theatrical expression.

Roaming through Athens: A Timeless Experience

As you explore these iconic facets of Athens, you embark on a journey that transcends time. The Acropolis, with its awe-inspiring temples, invites you to witness the splendor of the Golden Age. The Parthenon's architectural magnificence reflects the triumphs of human creativity. The Agora stands as a testament to democratic ideals and the power of philosophical discourse. The National Archaeological Museum preserves the treasures that narrate Greece's millennia-spanning narrative. Plaka offers a glimpse into the city's old-world charm. The Theatre of Dionysus unearths the origins of dramatic storytelling.

Roaming through Athens is not just a tourist experience; it's an immersive encounter with history, culture, and the enduring legacy of a civilization that shaped the world. Each step you take carries you closer to the heartbeat of antiquity, where gods, philosophers, and citizens once converged, leaving an indelible mark on the tapestry of human existence. In Athens, history truly comes alive, and the past continues to resonate in the present.

The Enigmatic Ruins of Ephesus

Nestled within the lush landscapes of modern-day Turkey, the ancient city of Ephesus emerges as a living testament to the grandeur of civilizations long past. As you step foot upon this hallowed ground, an ethereal aura surrounds you, whisking you away to an era of unparalleled architectural achievements, profound cultural exchanges, and remarkable historical significance. The enigmatic ruins of Ephesus offer not only a glimpse into the past but also an immersive experience that transcends time itself.

Historical Significance: Tracing the Footsteps of the Ages

Ephesus, a bustling port city that once thrived as a center of trade, religion, and scholarship, occupies a pivotal position in the tapestry of the ancient world. Its origins can be traced back to the Hellenistic period, but it was during the Roman era that Ephesus truly flourished, ascending to the status of a metropolis. Positioned strategically along the Aegean coast, the city's prosperity was deeply entwined with its role as a hub for trade routes connecting Asia Minor to distant corners of the Roman Empire. The bustling streets of Ephesus bore witness to the exchange of goods, ideas, and cultures that enriched its character.

Architectural Marvels: Sculpting Stone into Dreams

One of the most iconic and revered structures that grace the landscape of Ephesus is the Library of Celsus. A masterpiece of ancient architecture, this awe-inspiring monument stands as a testament to human ingenuity and dedication. Its facade, intricately adorned with delicate carvings and statues, enveloped the repository of thousands of scrolls and manuscripts, earning its place among the most revered libraries of the ancient world. As you stand before this grand edifice, it's impossible not to feel the weight of the knowledge it once safeguarded.

The Great Theater of Ephesus, another architectural marvel, demands attention with its colossal presence. Capable of accommodating up to 25,000 spectators, this monumental theater served as the epicenter of cultural and social events. The air here once reverberated with the sounds of riveting theatrical performances, impassioned speeches, and the collective energy of a community united by art and discourse.

The Temple of Artemis: A Beacon of Worship and Wonder

Among the many wonders that Ephesus offered, one stood above all others: the Temple of Artemis. Revered as one of the Seven Wonders of the Ancient World, this temple stood as a testament to the devotion of the people and the brilliance of human craftsmanship. Although little remains of the temple today, its significance in the realms of culture, religion, and architecture is unparalleled. Dedicated to Artemis, the Greek goddess of the hunt and wilderness, this monumental structure drew pilgrims and visitors from far and wide, leaving an indelible mark on the annals of history.

Walking Through Time: Echoes of Lives Lived

As you traverse the ancient streets of Ephesus, the remnants of grand villas, public baths, and intricate mosaics beckon you to immerse yourself in the daily lives of its inhabitants. The Marble Street, a magnificent thoroughfare paved with pristine white marble, stands as a testament to the opulence that defined the city's urban planning. In its heyday, this street witnessed a multitude of life's experiences, from the mundane to the momentous, echoing with the footsteps of generations.

The Terrace Houses, an enclave of elegantly adorned residences, provide a privileged window into the lives of Ephesus' affluent residents. Within these finely crafted homes, frescoes painted with meticulous care, intricate tile work, and indoor plumbing systems offer a tantalizing glimpse into the advanced lifestyle of the time. These houses are not merely ruins; they are the echoes of lives once lived, stories once told, and legacies once forged.

Preserving the Past: Guardians of History

The enigmatic ruins of Ephesus have been meticulously excavated, studied, and preserved over the years. As visitors step onto this hallowed ground, they're not just encountering the remains of a bygone era; they're immersing themselves in a living history. The arduous efforts to safeguard and restore these ruins have transformed Ephesus into a time capsule, transporting us to an era when empires rose and fell, and the course of human civilization was shaped.

Visiting Ephesus Today: Time Travelers of the Modern Age

In the present day, Ephesus beckons history enthusiasts, archaeology aficionados, and curious travelers with its allure. Guided tours and interpretive signage act as portals, bridging the gap between past and present, allowing visitors to fathom the significance of each structure and the role it played in the city's narrative. As you tread the worn cobblestones of Ephesus, you're not just exploring ruins; you're engaging with the stories etched into its stone foundations. You're hearing the whispers of conversations that took place centuries ago, and you're retracing the footsteps that once echoed through its bustling streets.

The journey through the enigmatic ruins of Ephesus is a journey through time itself. It's a journey that awakens a profound sense of connection to the past and offers a humbling perspective on the continuum of human existence. It's a reminder that while empires may rise and fall, the echoes of their achievements, aspirations, and dreams persist, forever etched into the stones they left behind.

Spain's Iberian Peninsula - A Journey of Contrasts

Barcelona's Modernist Treasures

Barcelona, the vibrant capital of Catalonia, Spain, is renowned for its unique and captivating architecture. One of the city's most iconic and distinctive periods in architecture is Modernism, also known as Art Nouveau. Emerging in the late 19th and early 20th centuries, Modernism in Barcelona was heavily influenced by the Catalan architectural genius Antoni Gaudí and his contemporaries.

La Sagrada Família: The Crown Jewel of Modernism

At the heart of the bustling city of Barcelona stands a towering masterpiece that has captured the imagination of millions - the Sagrada Família. This basilica, a symbol of Barcelona and one of the most famous works of architect Antoni Gaudí, embodies the spirit of Modernism, transcending its architectural category to become a spiritual and artistic monument.

The Vision and Construction

The saga of the Sagrada Família began in 1882 when Gaudí took over its design, intending to create a temple that would honor the Holy Family (Sagrada Família in Spanish) in a way that harmonized with nature. The project's grand scale and complexity meant that Gaudí dedicated much of his life to it. He not only meticulously designed the basilica but also drew inspiration from nature, geometry, and his religious beliefs to craft an architectural marvel unlike any other.

Organic Forms and Intricate Facades

What makes the Sagrada Família so exceptional is its fusion of Gothic and Modernist elements, resulting in a unique architectural language. The basilica's facades are adorned with intricate sculptures and symbolic details that tell the story of Jesus Christ's life. The Nativity Façade, the first to be completed, exudes a sense of birth, life, and rebirth, with its detailed depictions of nativity scenes and life-sized sculptures.

Moving towards the Passion Façade, the tone changes dramatically. Gaudí's intention was to convey the intensity of Christ's suffering through sharp lines and stark sculptures. This part of the basilica is an embodiment of raw emotion, making visitors pause and reflect on the sacrifice it represents.

Stunning Interior and Play of Light

Step inside the Sagrada Família, and you'll be enveloped by a breathtaking interplay of light and color. The basilica's columns soar like trees, branching out to support the awe-inspiring ceiling. Gaudí's ingenious use of a hyperboloid structure allows for the dispersion of light in all directions, creating a serene, otherworldly atmosphere. The stained glass windows, which vary in color and intensity, cast a spectrum of hues onto the interior, transforming the space into a spiritual kaleidoscope.

A Legacy in Progress

One of the most intriguing aspects of the Sagrada Família is its ongoing construction. Gaudí passed away in 1926, leaving behind only a fraction of the basilica's intended design. However, his vision has lived on through generations of architects, artists, and craftsmen. The continued construction has also sparked debates about the balance between honoring Gaudí's original ideas and incorporating contemporary architectural techniques.

As of today, the basilica remains a work in progress, with an estimated completion date in the 2030s. The journey to complete the Sagrada Família has been a testament to human dedication and perseverance, much like the artistic and spiritual journeys it has inspired in its countless visitors.

A Spiritual Oasis in the Urban Jungle

The Sagrada Família is not merely a structure; it's a living testament to faith, art, and architecture's boundless potential. As you stand beneath its towering spires, you can't help but be struck by the sheer ambition and dedication that have gone into its creation. This basilica is a beacon of spirituality in the midst of the urban hustle, inviting visitors to contemplate the intersection of the divine and the human.

The Sagrada Família has become an emblem of Barcelona, attracting pilgrims, artists, architects, and tourists from around the globe. Its ongoing construction ensures that Gaudí's dream and vision continue to evolve, making the basilica not only a celebration of Modernism but a living embodiment of creativity and human ingenuity.

Casa Batlló: A House of Curves and Colors

On the renowned Passeig de Gràcia in Barcelona, stands a building that defies convention and redefines architectural aesthetics - Casa Batlló. Crafted by the visionary architect Antoni Gaudí, this residential masterpiece is a testament to his distinctive Modernist approach, characterized by its undulating forms, vibrant mosaics, and fluid lines.

A Creative Transformation

Built between 1904 and 1906, Casa Batlló was originally a conventional apartment building. However, when Josep Batlló acquired the property, he commissioned Gaudí to transform it into something extraordinary. Gaudí's imaginative mind conceived a space where architecture and art merged seamlessly, transcending functional design to become an expression of beauty and innovation.

The Facade: Waves of Inspiration

The most striking feature of Casa Batlló is undoubtedly its facade. Gaudí employed his signature style of "trencadís," a mosaic technique using broken ceramic pieces, to create a facade that resembles the scales of a dragon. This earned the building its local nickname, Casa dels Ossos (House of Bones). The curvature of the facade is akin to the undulating waves of the sea, while the colors evoke the vibrant hues of marine life.

The Interior: An Immersive Artistic Experience

Entering Casa Batlló is akin to stepping into a surreal dreamscape. Gaudí's organic design principles are on full display as you encounter flowing lines, curved ceilings, and carefully crafted details that mimic natural forms. The central light well, with its skylight and blue ceramic tiles, resembles an underwater oasis, bathing the interior with soft, diffused light.

The Noble Floor: A World of Elegance

Casa Batlló's noble floor, where the Batlló family once resided, is a celebration of opulence and refinement. The rooms are a harmonious blend of functionality and artistry. The wooden paneling, stained glass windows, and intricate details create an ambiance that's both inviting and regal. One of the highlights is the "Gallery of Bones," an arched hallway adorned with sculpted columns that seem to dance.

The Roof: Dragon's Back and Chimneys

Casa Batlló's roof is a playground of imagination. Gaudí designed it to resemble the spine of a dragon, with multi-colored tiles and undulating forms. The roof is punctuated by whimsical chimney stacks that resemble fantastical creatures. This space is a true testament to Gaudí's ability to infuse even the most utilitarian elements with creativity and artistic flair.

Casa Batlló's Legacy and Impact

Casa Batlló is more than a building; it's a testament to Gaudí's ability to transform architecture into art. Its influence has transcended time, inspiring generations of architects and artists to embrace creativity, innovation, and a harmonious integration with nature. The building's status as a UNESCO World Heritage Site underscores its significance as a cultural and architectural treasure.

Visiting Casa Batlló is an immersive experience that transcends the visual and engages the senses on a profound level. As you explore its rooms, wander through its hallways, and gaze at its intricate details, you're invited into Gaudí's world of imagination and beauty. Casa Batlló stands as a testament to the limitless potential of architecture to inspire awe and spark the fires of creativity in all who encounter it.

Park Güell: Nature and Architecture in Harmony

Perched atop Carmel Hill, overlooking the bustling city of Barcelona, lies a whimsical oasis that blurs the lines between architecture and nature - Park Güell. Conceived by the visionary architect Antoni Gaudí, this public park is a testament to his profound understanding of both organic forms and innovative design.

A Garden City Vision

Commissioned by Count Eusebi Güell, the park was originally intended to be a garden city, a residential complex inspired by the English garden cities of the time. However, the project was never fully realized as a residential area, and it was eventually transformed into a public park. Gaudí's concept aimed to harmonize urban living with the natural world, creating a space where art and nature coexist in perfect balance.

Organic Architecture Unleashed

The most iconic feature of Park Güell is the Main Terrace, a sprawling area adorned with colorful mosaics, serpentine benches, and whimsical sculptures. Gaudí's use of organic shapes is evident in every element, from the undulating lines of the benches to the mosaic-covered salamander known as

"El Drac." The terrace is a celebration of curves, colors, and the tactile experience, inviting visitors to engage with the space on a sensory level.

The Hypostyle Room: A Forest of Columns

Venturing deeper into the park, visitors encounter the Hypostyle Room, a space that feels like a forest of slender, Doric-inspired columns. These columns support the terrace above, creating a sense of grandeur and intimacy simultaneously. The ceiling is adorned with a mosaic sun, a testament to Gaudí's fascination with natural symbols and celestial bodies.

Gaudí's House-Museum: Insight into Creativity

Within the park, Gaudí's former residence is now a museum that offers insight into his creative process. The house is a prime example of Gaudí's distinctive architectural style, with its decorative elements, imaginative use of materials, and integration with the surrounding landscape. Visiting Gaudí's house provides a glimpse into the mind of a genius and the artistic principles that shaped Park Güell.

The Serpentine Bench: A Seat of Delight

One of the most enchanting features of Park Güell is the Serpentine Bench, a sinuous structure that winds along the edge of the Main Terrace. Covered in mosaic tiles, the bench is not only a functional seating area but also an artistic marvel. Its curvature, colors, and tactile design invite visitors to pause, interact, and enjoy panoramic views of the city and the Mediterranean Sea.

Park Güell's Enduring Legacy

Park Güell's influence extends far beyond its physical boundaries. Its innovative approach to urban planning, its celebration of nature, and its seamless integration of art into public spaces have left an indelible mark on the world of architecture and design. The park's role as a UNESCO World Heritage Site underscores its cultural and historical significance, ensuring that Gaudí's vision continues to inspire generations of visitors and creators.

Visiting Park Güell is an immersive experience that awakens the senses and ignites the imagination. As you wander through its pathways, sit on its benches, and marvel at its architectural wonders, you become part of Gaudí's vision of a world where art and nature coalesce in harmonious splendor. Park Güell is a testament to the enduring power of creative expression and the boundless potential of the human spirit.

Casa Milà (La Pedrera): Sculptural Elegance

In the heart of Barcelona, an architectural marvel stands as a testament to innovation, creativity, and the limitless possibilities of design - Casa Milà, often referred to as La Pedrera. Crafted by the visionary architect Antoni Gaudí, Casa Milà defies convention, reimagining the concept of a residential building as a sculptural masterpiece that blurs the boundaries between art and architecture.

An Unconventional Vision

Commissioned by Pere Milà and his wife Roser Segimon, Casa Milà was constructed between 1906 and 1912. Gaudí's vision was rooted in his belief that architecture should transcend mere functionality and embrace artistic expression. This philosophy is evident in every facet of Casa

Milà, from its undulating façade to its innovative ventilation and lighting systems.

The Facade: Waves of Stone

Approaching Casa Milà, the first impression is one of awe and curiosity. The undulating stone facade, devoid of traditional right angles, appears as if shaped by the hands of nature. This organic design philosophy, a hallmark of Gaudí's work, creates an ever-changing interplay of light and shadow, lending the building a dynamic, living quality.

Innovative Structural Solutions

Casa Milà's structure is equally revolutionary. Instead of relying on load-bearing walls, Gaudí employed a system of self-supporting stone columns and floor slabs. This innovation not only allowed for more open interior spaces but also facilitated the creation of uniquely shaped rooms, each with its own character and purpose.

The Inner Courtyard: An Oasis of Light

Venturing into the inner courtyard, visitors are greeted by a space bathed in natural light. Gaudí's innovative approach to illumination is showcased through the use of strategically placed windows, creating a gentle, diffused glow that permeates the building's core. The central well is adorned with wrought iron railings that resemble sea waves, a nod to Casa Milà's maritime inspiration.

The Roof: An Artistic Dreamscape

Perhaps one of the most iconic features of Casa Milà is its rooftop. Here, Gaudí's imaginative spirit takes flight as sculptural chimneys, ventilation shafts, and staircases create a surreal landscape reminiscent of an otherworldly terrain. The rooftop is a space of artistic experimentation, where functional elements are transformed into works of art that delight the senses and ignite the imagination.

Espai Gaudí: A Glimpse into Genius

Casa Milà's top floor, known as Espai Gaudí, is dedicated to the life and work of Antoni Gaudí. This exhibition space offers visitors a comprehensive insight into Gaudí's creative process, showcasing his sketches, models, and architectural innovations. The exhibition not only provides a deeper understanding of Casa Milà but also offers a glimpse into the mind of a visionary genius.

Casa Milà's Enduring Significance

Casa Milà's legacy extends far beyond its role as a residential building. It is a symbol of Gaudí's architectural brilliance, a testament to his ability to challenge norms, and an embodiment of his belief that architecture should be a form of artistic expression. The building's designation as a UNESCO World Heritage Site further underscores its cultural and historical importance.

Visiting Casa Milà is a journey into a world where architectural boundaries are pushed, where functional spaces become works of art, and where innovation and creativity converge. As you explore its corridors, ascend its staircases, and gaze upon its sculpted forms, you become a part of Gaudí's vision, a vision that continues to inspire architects, artists, and dreamers around the world.

Palau de la Música Catalana: Music in Architectural Harmony

In the heart of Barcelona's historic district, a symphony of architecture and music unfolds in a breathtaking harmony - the Palau de la Música Catalana. Designed by the visionary architect Lluís Domènech i Montaner, this concert hall is not only a magnificent venue for musical performances but also a celebration of light, color, and artistic expression.

A Cultural Jewel

Constructed between 1905 and 1908, the Palau de la Música Catalana was envisioned as a space that would honor Catalonia's cultural heritage while embracing the artistic trends of the time. Domènech i Montaner's design marries various architectural styles, including Modernisme, Catalan Art Nouveau, and Gothic Revival, resulting in a structure that is both timeless and unique.

The Facade: A Kaleidoscope of Color

Approaching the Palau de la Música Catalana, visitors are greeted by a facade adorned with intricate sculptures, mosaics, and ornate detailing. The facade is a vibrant canvas that pays homage to Catalonia's artistic and cultural heritage. A central allegorical sculpture of Orpheus, the mythical musician and poet, stands as a symbol of the power of music to transcend earthly limitations.

The Stained Glass Skylight: A Symphony of Light

The heart of the Palau de la Música Catalana is its main concert hall, where music and architecture unite in breathtaking harmony. The focal point of the hall is the stunning stained glass skylight, which serves as both an artistic masterpiece and a practical source of illumination. Designed by the artist Antoni Rigalt i Blanch, the skylight casts a mesmerizing spectrum of colors onto the hall's interior, creating an ethereal ambiance that enhances the musical experience.

Organic Design Elements

Domènech i Montaner's design philosophy is characterized by its emphasis on natural forms and ornamentation. Throughout the Palau de la Música Catalana, floral motifs, intricate ironwork, and decorative elements inspired by nature abound. The use of organic shapes creates a sense of fluidity and movement, infusing the space with a dynamic energy that mirrors the vitality of music itself.

The Sculptures and Mosaics: Celebrating Creativity

The interior of the Palau de la Música Catalana is a sensory feast. Elaborate sculptures, mosaics, and ornate detailing adorn every surface, creating an immersive environment that stimulates the imagination. The central skylight is surrounded by a decorative halo of sculpted allegorical figures, paying homage to the performing arts and the creative spirit.

A Place of Artistic Convergence

Beyond its architectural splendor, the Palau de la Música Catalana holds a special place in the hearts of musicians, artists, and audiences. The concert hall has hosted a myriad of performances, from classical symphonies to contemporary compositions. Its acoustics are renowned for their clarity and resonance, ensuring that every note played within its walls reaches the hearts of those who listen.

A Legacy of Inspiration

The Palau de la Música Catalana stands as a testament to the enduring power of artistic expression. It is a space where architecture and music intertwine, where creativity finds a physical form, and where cultural heritage is celebrated. Its designation as a UNESCO World Heritage Site underscores its significance as a cultural treasure that continues to inspire and enchant audiences from around the world.

Visiting the Palau de la Música Catalana is an invitation to experience the magic of music in a setting that is as visually stunning as it is acoustically exceptional. As you sit in its hallowed hall, surrounded by mosaics, sculptures, and the play of light, you become a part of a tradition that celebrates the boundless potential of human creativity and the profound impact of artistic collaboration.

Andalusia's Moorish Heritage

Andalusia, a region in southern Spain, holds a rich and captivating Moorish heritage that dates back to the Middle Ages. The Moors, a group of Muslim peoples of North African origin, made a significant impact on the culture, architecture, and history of Andalusia during their rule that lasted for centuries.

The Alhambra Palace: Crown Jewel of Andalusia's Moorish Legacy

At the crossroads of history and architectural brilliance, the Alhambra Palace emerges as the crowning jewel of Andalusia's Moorish legacy. Perched majestically atop a hill overlooking the city of Granada, this UNESCO World Heritage site stands as a testament to the opulence, sophistication, and innovation of Moorish design that has withstood the test of time.

Architectural Marvel and Opulent Splendor

As visitors approach the Alhambra, they are greeted by an intricate tapestry of geometric patterns and intricate detailing that adorns the walls and facades. The palace complex unfolds as a labyrinthine treasure trove of exquisite craftsmanship, where every nook and cranny seems to whisper stories of a bygone era. The architecture is a symphony of mathematical precision and aesthetic beauty, as seen in the meticulously carved stucco, arabesque motifs, and calligraphic inscriptions that adorn the walls.

Enchanting Courtyards and Serene Fountains

Within the Alhambra's embrace, visitors are transported to a realm of tranquility and beauty. Serene courtyards, adorned with gardens and glistening fountains, offer a respite from the world outside. The Court of the Lions, nestled within the Nasrid Palaces, is an embodiment of paradise on earth. Its central fountain, supported by twelve marble lions, symbolizes strength and power. The intricate interplay of light and shadow, facilitated by the lattice screens and intricate windows, creates an almost otherworldly atmosphere that invites contemplation.

Nasrid Palaces: Fusion of Cultures and Styles

The Nasrid Palaces, with their delicate arches, ornate ceilings, and stately halls, embody the fusion of Islamic, Arabic, and Andalusian architectural sensibilities. The Palace of the Lions features a breathtaking dome adorned with star-shaped skylights, giving rise to an illusion of a celestial canopy. The Palace of the Partal, overlooking the reflecting pool and gardens, presents a harmonious balance between architecture and nature. Each palace tells a story of the intricate dance between form and function, aesthetics and purpose.

A Glimpse of the Celestial: Hall of the Abencerrajes

The Hall of the Abencerrajes is an embodiment of celestial beauty that leaves visitors spellbound. Its domed ceiling, adorned with intricate honeycomb-like patterns, guides the gaze towards a central star-shaped opening that seems to connect heaven and earth. Legend has it that this hall witnessed a tragic event involving the Abencerrajes family, further adding to its mystique. Standing within this hall evokes a sense of reverence and wonder, reminding us of the indomitable spirit of the Moors' artistic vision.

The Alhambra Palace encapsulates the essence of Andalusia's Moorish heritage, a testament to human ingenuity and the fusion of cultures. It stands not only as an architectural marvel but also as a gateway to a world where art, culture, and history intertwine in a captivating tapestry. As the Alhambra continues to stand tall, it beckons travelers from around the world to immerse themselves in its beauty and experience the legacy of the Moors that has left an indelible mark on the cultural landscape of Andalusia.

Cordoba's Mesmerizing Mezquita-Catedral

In the heart of Cordoba, another captivating chapter of Andalusia's Moorish heritage unfolds within the walls of the Mezquita-Catedral. This architectural marvel is a living embodiment of the region's complex history, where layers of cultures and faiths are interwoven to create a space of profound beauty and significance.

A Fusion of Styles: From Mosque to Cathedral

The Mezquita-Catedral is a unique blend of architectural styles that reflects the evolution of Cordoba's history. Its origins trace back to the 8th century when the Umayyad Caliphate constructed the Great Mosque of Cordoba. The mosque's vast prayer hall, supported by an astonishing array of horseshoe arches and columns, presents an awe-inspiring sight. The repetition of these arches creates a sense of rhythm and harmony, transporting visitors into a world of intricate geometry and serenity.

Harmonious Coexistence of Cultures

The conversion of the mosque into a cathedral following the Reconquista introduced elements of Gothic, Renaissance, and Baroque styles, underscoring the coexistence of diverse cultures within the same space. The insertion of the Cathedral's nave into the mosque's center is a visual representation of the integration of faiths. The juxtaposition of Christian chapels against the backdrop of Moorish arches exemplifies the harmonious coexistence of two distinct cultural identities.

Reflections in the Mihrab and Patio de los Naranjos

One of the Mezquita-Catedral's most iconic features is the mihrab, a semi-circular niche that indicates the direction of prayer in Islam. The intricate mosaics and ornate detailing of the mihrab reflect the deep reverence of the Umayyad period for art and spirituality. The Patio de los Naranjos, or Courtyard of the Orange Trees, with its rows of citrus trees and fountains, provides a tranquil setting for contemplation, further enriching the spiritual experience of the mosque.

A Testament to Heritage and Tolerance

The Mezquita-Catedral stands not only as an architectural masterpiece but also as a symbol of religious tolerance and cultural exchange. It serves as a reminder of the passage of time, the ebb and flow of history, and the ability of architecture to capture the essence of human experience. The interplay between light and shadow, the juxtaposition of cultures, and the layers of history make the Mezquita-Catedral a space of profound significance, inviting visitors to reflect on the shared heritage that shapes Andalusia's identity.

In exploring the Mezquita-Catedral, travelers embark on a journey through time, witnessing the transformation of a place of worship into a testament of unity and diversity. The Mezquita-Catedral's walls echo with the prayers of generations and the footsteps of diverse pilgrims, making it an enduring symbol of Andalusia's cultural richness and the enduring legacy of the Moors.

The Alcazar of Seville: A Palatial Marvel

Nestled within the heart of Seville, the Alcazar stands as a testament to the Moors' architectural prowess and the enduring legacy of their influence. This royal palace, characterized by its intricate design and cultural fusion, offers a captivating glimpse into the rich tapestry of Andalusia's history and artistic heritage.

A Fusion of Styles and Cultures

The Alcazar seamlessly weaves together Islamic, Mudéjar, and Christian influences, creating a captivating visual symphony that resonates with visitors. As you step into the palace complex, you are immediately greeted by a harmonious blend of delicate arches, intricate tilework, and lush gardens. This blending of artistic traditions echoes the spirit of unity in diversity that defines Andalusia's cultural landscape.

Patio de las Doncellas: Courtyard of Elegance

One of the Alcazar's most enchanting features is the Patio de las Doncellas, the Courtyard of the Maidens. This courtyard, framed by arches and adorned with ornate tilework, encapsulates the essence of Mudéjar architecture. The tranquil reflecting pool at its center creates a sense of serenity and symmetry. The architectural details speak of an era when aesthetics and functionality were intertwined, resulting in spaces that inspire wonder and reflection.

Gardens of Eden: Paradise on Earth

Beyond the palatial halls, the Alcazar's gardens offer a glimpse into the paradisiacal beauty often described in Islamic literature. The meticulously designed gardens feature an array of plant species, vibrant flowerbeds, and intricate water features. Strolling through these gardens, one can't help but feel transported to a realm of tranquility, where the interplay of light and shadow creates a sense of magic and serenity.

A Living Heritage and Cultural Nexus

The Alcazar's legacy extends beyond its architectural grandeur. Its walls have borne witness to centuries of history, serving as a backdrop for diplomatic negotiations, royal ceremonies, and artistic endeavors. It's not just a relic of the past; it's a living testament to the enduring impact of the Moors' vision and creativity.

Unveiling the Past, Embracing the Future

Exploring the Alcazar is a journey through time, where the intricate tile mosaics, intricate ceilings, and lush gardens whisper tales of the past. The Alcazar's continued preservation stands as a commitment to honor the legacy of the Moors and to ensure that future generations can continue to be captivated by its beauty and historical significance. As visitors step into the Alcazar, they step into a realm where history, art, and culture converge, inviting them to be a part of the ongoing narrative of Andalusia's rich heritage.

Influence on Art, Music, and Culture

Andalusia's Moorish heritage extends far beyond its architectural wonders, permeating the very essence of the region's art, music, literature, and cultural identity. This influence is a vibrant thread woven into the fabric of

Andalusia, enriching its cultural tapestry and contributing to its unique allure.

Inspiring Artistry: Geometric Patterns and Arabesque Motifs

The intricate geometric patterns and arabesque motifs that adorn the walls of the Alhambra, Mezquita-Catedral, and Alcazar have served as wellsprings of inspiration for artists across generations. These designs, characterized by their mathematical precision and harmonious symmetry, have influenced various art forms, from painting and sculpture to textiles and ceramics. Artists have drawn upon these patterns to infuse their creations with a sense of elegance, balance, and aesthetic depth.

Rhythms of Flamenco: Moorish Origins

Flamenco, the soul-stirring musical and dance tradition synonymous with Andalusia, owes some of its origins to the Moors. It's believed that the rhythmic patterns, melodic scales, and passionate expressiveness found in Flamenco have roots in North African musical traditions. The fusion of diverse musical influences, including Moorish, Gypsy, Jewish, and Spanish, has given rise to a genre that resonates with emotion, capturing the essence of Andalusia's cultural fusion.

Literary Echoes: Tales of Andalusian Splendor

The enchanting allure of Andalusia's Moorish heritage has also found its way into literature. Poets and writers have been captivated by the region's architectural wonders, the interplay of cultures, and the timeless beauty that resonates from the Alhambra's walls and the Alcazar's gardens. The intricate architectural details and the captivating narratives of the past have inspired stories and poems that transport readers into the heart of Andalusia's cultural landscape.

Culinary Traditions: Fusion of Flavors

Even the culinary traditions of Andalusia bear the imprint of Moorish influence. The introduction of ingredients like rice, almonds, citrus fruits, and spices reflects the historical exchanges between cultures. Dishes like "paella," with its rich blend of flavors, and "almond-based desserts" pay homage to the culinary legacy of the Moors. The region's gastronomy is a delectable testament to the enduring impact of their presence.

Preserving the Past for the Future

Andalusia's Moorish heritage is not confined to the annals of history; it thrives in the present, shaping the identity and character of the region. Efforts to preserve and restore these architectural wonders, coupled with the continued celebration of art, music, and cultural traditions, ensure that the Moors' legacy remains vibrant and relevant. The Alhambra, the Mezquita-Catedral, the Alcazar, and the broader cultural heritage they represent are living expressions of Andalusia's commitment to honoring its past while embracing its future.

In embracing Andalusia's Moorish heritage, travelers embark on a journey that transcends time, immersing themselves in a world of artistic expression, cultural exchange, and historical significance. From the graceful arches of the Alhambra to the rhythmic beats of Flamenco, the influence of the Moors is a treasure trove that continues to inspire, captivate, and enrich the region's cultural narrative.

Chapter 2: The Mediterranean Mosaic - Culture and Traditions

Festivals and Celebrations

The Mediterranean region is known for its vibrant and lively festivals that showcase the rich cultural tapestry of the various countries that line its shores. These celebrations are a reflection of the region's history, traditions, and the strong sense of community that binds its people together. In this chapter, we will delve into two of the most iconic festivals that take place in the Mediterranean – "La Tomatina" in Spain and "The Carnival of Venice" in Italy. These festivals are not only a feast for the senses but also provide a unique opportunity for travelers to immerse themselves in the local culture and experience the joyous spirit of the Mediterranean firsthand.

La Tomatina: Spain's Tomato-Flinging Fiesta

Every year on the last Wednesday of August, the small town of Buñol in the Valencia region of Spain transforms into a riotous sea of red as thousands of participants gather for "La Tomatina." This unconventional festival, which has gained international fame, centers around a massive tomato fight where participants pelt each other with overripe tomatoes, turning the streets into a red-hued battleground of tomato pulp.

The origins of La Tomatina are somewhat unclear, with various stories attributing its beginnings to a food fight among friends or a protest against the town council. Regardless of its origins, the festival has evolved into a symbol of fun, camaraderie, and a unique way to celebrate life. The event kicks off with the "palo jabón," a greased pole with a ham placed at the top. Participants compete to climb the pole and claim the ham, marking the start of the tomato fight.

As the signal is given, trucks laden with tomatoes arrive, and the streets become a frenzy of flying tomatoes, laughter, and excitement. Locals and tourists alike join in the chaos, throwing tomatoes at friends and strangers with gleeful abandon. The tomato fight lasts for about an hour, after which the streets are washed down by fire trucks, leaving behind a striking tableau of red-stained buildings and satisfied participants.

The Carnival of Venice: Masks, Music, and Magic

The enchanting city of Venice comes alive every year in the weeks leading up to Lent during the Carnival of Venice, a centuries-old celebration that harks back to the city's extravagant past. Known for its opulent masks, elaborate costumes, and grand masquerade balls, the Carnival of Venice is a time when the city's narrow streets and historic squares transform into a stage for breathtaking displays of creativity and artistry.

The origins of the Carnival can be traced back to the 12th century, when Venetians would gather to indulge in feasting and revelry before the austere period of Lent began. As the centuries passed, the Carnival evolved into a grand affair marked by lavish parties, parades, and masked balls. The masks, in particular, have become an integral part of the

Carnival's identity, allowing wearers to assume different personas and indulge in a sense of anonymity.

One of the highlights of the Carnival is the "Flight of the Angel," a tradition that involves a person descending on a zipline from the iconic St. Mark's Campanile to the center of St. Mark's Square. This symbolic act marks the beginning of the festivities and is accompanied by a colorful parade of participants dressed in exquisite costumes and masks. Throughout the Carnival, the city is abuzz with musical performances, theater shows, and culinary delights, creating an atmosphere of enchantment and celebration.

Fallas: A Fiery Spectacle in Valencia, Spain

The city of Valencia in Spain is renowned for hosting one of the most visually spectacular festivals in the Mediterranean – "Las Fallas." Held annually from March 15 to 19, this event is a dazzling showcase of elaborate sculptures, vibrant parades, and a grand display of fireworks that light up the night sky.

The origins of Fallas date back to a tradition among carpenters who used to burn their wooden shavings and discarded materials on the feast day of Saint Joseph, the patron saint of carpenters. Over time, this practice evolved into the creation of intricate, towering sculptures known as "fallas." These sculptures often satirize current events, politics, and societal issues, and they are meticulously crafted over months.

The climax of Fallas is "La Cremà," the burning of the fallas on the night of March 19. As the sculptures, some of which can reach several stories in height, are set ablaze, the city is bathed in a fiery glow and the air is filled with the scent of smoke. It's a bittersweet moment, as these incredible works of art are transformed into ashes, symbolizing the impermanence of life.

Fête de la Musique: Melodies in the Streets of Nice, France

On June 21st each year, the charming streets of Nice, France, come alive with the joyful sounds of music during "Fête de la Musique." Translated as the "Festival of Music," this event celebrates the summer solstice and the universal language of music. Musicians of all genres and skill levels take to the streets, parks, and squares to share their talents with the public, creating a magical ambiance that resonates throughout the city.

Originating in France in 1982, the Fête de la Musique quickly spread to other countries, becoming an international phenomenon. In Nice, the festival is a true representation of the city's diverse musical scene, featuring performances that range from classical orchestras to contemporary rock bands, and everything in between. The streets become stages, and locals and tourists alike join in the festivities, dancing, singing, and appreciating the harmony that music brings.

What sets Fête de la Musique apart is its accessibility – the performances are free, and musicians of all ages and backgrounds are encouraged to participate. This inclusive spirit reflects the Mediterranean's celebration of togetherness and cultural exchange, as people from different walks of life come together through the universal language of music.

Festival of the Aegean: Harmonies on the Greek Islands

In the enchanting backdrop of the Greek Islands, the Festival of the Aegean emerges as a celebration of music, opera, and culture. Taking place annually in July, this festival is hosted on the island of Syros and draws both local and international talents to its stages. The Festival of the Aegean is a testimony to the region's artistic heritage, with performances ranging from classical music to contemporary compositions. Against the backdrop of cerulean waters and charming island architecture, attendees immerse themselves in the melodic harmonies that echo across the Aegean.

Cavalcade of Kings: Epiphany Celebrations in Tarpon Springs, Greece

In the small town of Tarpon Springs, Greece, a unique and deeply traditional event called the "Cavalcade of Kings" takes place every January 6th. This celebration marks the Feast of Epiphany, commemorating the baptism of Jesus Christ. A distinctive aspect of this event is the blessing of the waters. Following a solemn liturgy, a white cross is cast into the water, and young men dive in to retrieve it – a symbol of luck for the coming year. The event culminates in a grand parade featuring elaborately adorned horses and local community members dressed in traditional Greek attire. The Cavalcade of Kings is a testament to the enduring cultural ties between the Mediterranean and its diaspora, as Tarpon Springs holds the highest population of Greek-Americans in the United States.

Cannes Film Festival: A Glamorous Mediterranean Affair

While the Mediterranean is renowned for its traditional festivities, it also hosts one of the most prestigious modern events – the Cannes Film Festival. Held annually in the city of Cannes, France, this glamorous gathering is a celebration of international cinema. The red carpet is rolled out for a multitude of film screenings, premiers, and industry-related events. Celebrities, filmmakers, and cinephiles from around the world converge on the French Riviera to partake in this cinematic extravaganza. The Cannes Film Festival serves as a bridge between the Mediterranean's cultural heritage and its contemporary global influence, showcasing the region's ability to remain at the forefront of creativity and artistic expression.

Fiesta de San Juan: A Midsummer Night's Revelry in Spain

As the warm embrace of summer envelops the Mediterranean coastline of Spain, the skies alight with fire and the waves seem to dance in response. This magical transformation occurs during the celebrated Fiesta de San Juan, a night of revelry that takes place on the eve of June 23rd. Emerging from centuries-old traditions and echoing the essence of the summer solstice, this event is a harmonious fusion of fire, water, and shared merriment.

The Fiesta de San Juan marks the longest day of the year and the official arrival of summer. It also holds a special place in Spanish hearts as a tribute to St. John the Baptist, a figure symbolizing renewal and the transition into a season of warmth and vitality. As the sun dips below the horizon, cities, towns, and villages along the Mediterranean coast come alive with a captivating symphony of bonfires.

Beaches become amphitheaters of light as flames flicker, casting their golden glow upon the sands. In city squares and public spaces, these communal fires serve as beacons of tradition, marking the celestial dance of the sun and the earth. The bonfires symbolize not just the sun's energy but also its power to purify and renew, making them the heart of this enchanting celebration.

One of the most captivating traditions of the Fiesta de San Juan involves the daring act of jumping over the flames. As the bonfires crackle and send sparks into the night sky, locals and visitors alike gather around to partake in this ancient ritual. Jumping over the flames is believed to cleanse the spirit, ushering in good fortune and leaving behind any negativity. There's a sense of exhilaration as people leap through the fire, a mix of laughter and courage that creates a bond among those who share in the experience.

The festive atmosphere continues with live music that pulses through the air, infusing the night with energy and rhythm. Dancing feet move to the beat, transcending language barriers and cultural divides, as joy becomes the universal language. Amidst the sounds of celebration, traditional dishes are savored, and the aroma of grilled meats and seafood mingles with the sea breeze.

As the night deepens, the festivities remain unabated. Feasting continues, drinks flow, and laughter echoes under the star-studded sky. Friends and strangers become companions in celebration, drawn together by the desire to embrace life and honor the juncture of light and warmth.

The Fiesta de San Juan is more than a mere event; it's a moment when time seems suspended, and the boundaries between individuals blur in the embrace of shared joy. This celebration exemplifies the Mediterranean's unique ability to merge tradition and festivity, fire and water, ancient practices and modern camaraderie. As dawn approaches, and the fires slowly fade, the memories of this Midsummer Night's Revelry linger, forever connecting those who participated to the eternal dance of seasons and the enchanting spirit of Spain's Mediterranean coast.

Feast of the Assumption: Honoring the Virgin Mary in Italy

Amid the sun-kissed landscapes of Italy's Mediterranean coast, the heart and spirit of the nation converge in a celebration that blends devotion with festivity. August 15th, the Feast of the Assumption, is a day that holds a special place in the hearts of Italians. While this significant event is observed across the country, it takes on a particularly poignant character in the towns and villages that line the enchanting shores of the Mediterranean.

At the heart of this celebration lies a profound tribute to the Virgin Mary. The Feast of the Assumption commemorates her ascent into heaven, her purity, and her role as the spiritual mother of humanity. In towns along the coastline, the streets awaken with a palpable sense of reverence and unity as communities prepare to honor their spiritual heritage.

Ornate floats adorned with intricate statues of the Virgin Mary become the focal point of the celebrations. These floats are paraded through narrow cobblestone streets, creating a striking juxtaposition between the ancient buildings and the ethereal beauty of the sculptures. Each float tells a story, a testament to the skill and dedication of local artisans who have poured their hearts into creating these works of art.

The parades are a mesmerizing display of tradition and faith. Locals, dressed in traditional attire, march alongside the floats, and the air is filled with the sounds of music, chanting, and prayer. The parade route becomes a sacred path, with participants and observers alike drawn into a shared experience that transcends time.

The Feast of the Assumption is not solely a religious event; it's a celebration of community and culture. Colorful decorations adorn balconies and windows, creating a kaleidoscope of hues that mirrors the festive atmosphere. The spirit of togetherness is palpable, as families and friends gather to share in the joy of the occasion.

Music and dance envelop the streets, inviting everyone to partake in the festivities. Local musicians play traditional melodies that evoke a sense of nostalgia and pride, echoing through ancient alleyways and bustling piazzas. The aroma of traditional Italian cuisine wafts through the air, as food vendors offer delicacies that have been passed down through generations.

As the sun sets on this day of celebration, a deep sense of devotion and festivity lingers. The Feast of the Assumption is a poignant reminder of Italy's connection to its religious roots and the enduring cultural tapestry that has woven the nation's history. In the towns and villages along the Mediterranean, this event is a cherished tradition that encapsulates the essence of community, faith, and the enduring beauty of Italian culture.

Eid al-Fitr: Embracing Joy and Community in North Africa

As the golden rays of the Mediterranean sun herald a new day, the shores of North Africa come alive with an atmosphere of joy, unity, and gratitude. Eid al-Fitr, the Festival of Breaking the Fast, is a momentous occasion celebrated by Muslims across the world, and its vibrancy is particularly evident in the countries that grace the Mediterranean's edge, such as Morocco and Tunisia.

Eid al-Fitr marks the end of Ramadan, a month of fasting, prayer, and reflection. It's a time of spiritual renewal and connection, and the festival serves as a jubilant culmination of this period of devotion. The Mediterranean's role as a crossroads of cultures is evident in the unique way this festival is celebrated, blending religious significance with cultural traditions.

In the days leading up to Eid, homes and streets are adorned with decorations, infusing the air with a sense of excitement. Families come together to prepare special dishes, each with its own cultural nuances. Tables are laden with delicacies, ranging from sweet pastries to savory treats, reflecting the diversity of flavors that characterize the region.

One of the most endearing aspects of Eid al-Fitr is the exchange of gifts. From new clothes to heartfelt tokens, the act of giving symbolizes the spirit of generosity and kindness that defines this festival. Children eagerly await this moment, their eyes shining with anticipation as they receive tokens of love and affection from their elders.

The heart of Eid al-Fitr lies in communal prayer. Families gather in mosques and open spaces, their voices rising in unison as they offer prayers of gratitude and seek blessings for the future. The beauty of these moments transcends religious boundaries, underscoring the festival's universal message of unity and compassion.

Charitable acts are an integral part of Eid al-Fitr. Families extend invitations to neighbors, friends, and even strangers, ensuring that no one is left without a place at the table. Acts of kindness and charity reflect the core values of Islam and serve as a reminder of the importance of caring for one another.

As the sun sets, the festivities continue with communal feasts that stretch into the night. Laughter, music, and the clinking of glasses create a lively atmosphere, as people revel in the joy of the moment. The Mediterranean coastline becomes a tapestry of lights, a reflection of the shared happiness that radiates from every corner.

Eid al-Fitr in North Africa is a celebration that embraces both faith and culture. It's a testament to the region's deep-rooted values of togetherness, compassion, and gratitude. The Mediterranean becomes a stage for this display of joy, unity, and the eternal spirit of generosity that resonates through the hearts of those who partake in this cherished festival.

In essence, the Mediterranean's festivals and celebrations are a kaleidoscope of traditions, emotions, and creativity. From the harmonious notes of the Festival of the Aegean to the fervent celebrations of Epiphany in Tarpon Springs and the glitz of the Cannes Film Festival, these events continue to capture the essence of the Mediterranean spirit – vibrant, diverse, and deeply rooted in its heritage.

Art and Architecture

The Mediterranean region is a treasure trove of artistic and architectural wonders that bear witness to centuries of human creativity and cultural exchange. From the Renaissance splendors of Florence to the grandeur of Alhambra's Islamic architecture, this chapter delves into two remarkable destinations that showcase the enduring beauty and innovation of the Mediterranean's artistic heritage.

Renaissance Splendors in Florence

Nestled in the heart of Italy, Florence stands as a testament to the transformative power of the Renaissance era. Known as the "Cradle of the Renaissance," this enchanting city was a crucible of artistic, intellectual, and scientific advancements that swept across Europe during the 14th to 17th centuries.

One of the most iconic landmarks in Florence is the Florence Cathedral, commonly known as the Duomo. Its magnificent dome, designed by Filippo Brunelleschi, is a marvel of engineering and architecture. Visitors can climb to the top of the dome for panoramic views of the city's terracotta rooftops and the surrounding Tuscan hills.

The Uffizi Gallery, another gem of Florentine culture, houses an exceptional collection of Renaissance art. Paintings by renowned artists such as Leonardo da Vinci, Michelangelo, and Botticelli adorn the gallery's walls, offering a journey through the evolution of artistic styles during this period of rebirth.

Florence's Ponte Vecchio, a medieval bridge that spans the Arno River, is a living testament to the city's historical and architectural legacy. Lined with shops that have stood for centuries, it evokes a sense of timelessness and commerce that harks back to the Middle Ages.

The Grandeur of Alhambra's Islamic Architecture

Moving from the Italian Renaissance to the southern tip of Spain, we encounter the Alhambra, a breathtaking palace and fortress complex that encapsulates the beauty and sophistication of Islamic architecture. Situated on a hill overlooking the city of Granada, the Alhambra was built during the Nasrid dynasty's rule in the 13th century.

The Alhambra is a masterpiece of intricate geometric patterns, delicate stucco work, and meticulously designed gardens. Its Courtyard of the Lions is a prime example of Islamic architecture's emphasis on symmetry and symbolism. The courtyard features a central fountain supported by 12 marble lions, each representing a sign of the zodiac.

One of the most enchanting aspects of the Alhambra is the Generalife Gardens. These lush and serene gardens were designed as a place of relaxation for the Nasrid rulers. Terraced pathways, fountains, and pools are carefully integrated into the landscape, creating a harmonious connection between architecture and nature.

The Nasrid Palaces within the Alhambra complex offer a glimpse into the opulent lifestyle of the Moorish rulers. The Hall of the Abencerrajes features a stunning star-shaped dome, adorned with intricate muqarnas, a type of ornamental vaulting. The Palace of the Lions showcases the fusion of Islamic, Christian, and Jewish influences, underscoring the region's rich history of cultural exchange.

Sagrada Família: Gaudí's Unfinished Symphony in Barcelona

Barcelona, Spain, is home to one of the most awe-inspiring architectural marvels of the modern era – the Sagrada Família. Designed by the visionary architect Antoni Gaudí, this basilica is a testament to the fusion of Gothic and Art Nouveau styles. Construction began in 1882 and continues to this day, making it a perpetually evolving masterpiece.

The basilica's façades are adorned with intricate facades that depict various aspects of Christ's life and religious symbolism. The interior is a forest of columns that reach upwards like trees, supporting a ceiling that resembles a canopy of leaves and branches. Sunlight filtering through stained glass windows bathes the interior in a mesmerizing spectrum of colors, creating an ethereal and otherworldly ambiance.

Venice's Byzantine and Gothic Splendors

Venice, Italy, is renowned for its unique urban architecture that reflects the city's history as a maritime and cultural crossroads. The Byzantine and Gothic influences are particularly pronounced in its structures.

The Basilica di San Marco is a stunning example of Byzantine architecture, characterized by its intricate mosaics, domes, and opulent decoration. The façade is adorned with gold mosaics that depict biblical scenes and figures, creating a shimmering effect in the sunlight.

On the other hand, the Palazzo Ducale (Doge's Palace) showcases Venetian Gothic architecture. Its elegant arches, delicate tracery, and ornate balconies create a sense of airiness and grace. Inside, visitors can explore opulent chambers adorned with masterful paintings by artists like Tintoretto and Veronese.

Cappadocia's Cave Architecture

Moving to central Turkey, the region of Cappadocia presents a unique form of architecture that's intricately linked with the landscape. Cappadocia's ancient inhabitants carved homes, churches, and entire underground cities into the soft volcanic rock, resulting in a fascinating subterranean architectural wonder.

The Göreme Open-Air Museum is a prime example, showcasing rock-cut churches adorned with vibrant frescoes that depict scenes from the Bible. These churches offer insights into the spiritual and artistic life of the region's early Christian communities.

Malta's Megalithic Temples

Malta, an island nation in the Mediterranean, boasts some of the world's oldest free-standing structures – the Megalithic Temples. These prehistoric temples, built between 3600 and 2500 BCE, are older than the Egyptian pyramids and Stonehenge.

The temples, such as Ħaġar Qim and Mnajdra, are constructed using massive stone blocks, some of which weigh several tons. The precise alignment of these temples with celestial events suggests an advanced understanding of astronomy for their time.

Dubrovnik's Old Town: A Medieval Architectural Gem

Nestled along the Adriatic coast, Dubrovnik's Old Town in Croatia is a beautifully preserved example of medieval architecture. Encircled by towering walls and overlooking the shimmering blue sea, this UNESCO World Heritage Site transports visitors back in time.

The city walls themselves are a marvel of engineering and architecture, offering stunning panoramic views of the red-tiled rooftops and the azure waters beyond. Walking along these walls provides a unique perspective on the city's layout and the harmony between its buildings and natural surroundings.

Within the Old Town, the Rector's Palace stands as a testament to Dubrovnik's historical significance as a thriving maritime city-state. The palace's blend of Gothic, Renaissance, and Baroque elements reflects the city's evolving cultural influences over the centuries.

Marrakech's Intricate Moroccan Design

Venturing south to North Africa, Marrakech in Morocco beckons with its vibrant colors and intricate architecture. The city's medina (old city) is a maze of narrow alleys and bustling souks, where stunning architecture is intertwined with daily life.

The Bahia Palace showcases Moroccan craftsmanship at its finest, with its ornate stucco work, colorful tiles, and serene gardens. The Saadian Tombs, discovered in the early 20th century, are a hidden gem adorned with intricate carvings and mosaics.

Athens' Iconic Acropolis

No exploration of Mediterranean architecture would be complete without mentioning the Acropolis in Athens, Greece. Dominating the city's skyline, this ancient citadel boasts a collection of monumental structures that epitomize classical Greek architecture.

The Parthenon, dedicated to the goddess Athena, is a prime example of Doric architecture. Its graceful proportions, carefully calculated curvature, and intricate friezes are a testament to the Greeks' architectural prowess.

A Kaleidoscope of Architectural Marvels

The Mediterranean's architectural landscape is a kaleidoscope of styles, eras, and influences, reflecting the region's historical and cultural diversity. From the unfinished masterpiece of Gaudí's Sagrada Família to the intricate carvings of Cappadocia's cave dwellings, every architectural wonder tells a story of human creativity, ingenuity, and aspiration.

Whether you're captivated by the delicate stucco work of the Alhambra, the enduring elegance of Venice's Gothic architecture, or the ancient secrets of Malta's megalithic temples, the Mediterranean's art and architecture offer an extraordinary journey through time and culture. Each structure is a testament to the people who envisioned and built it, leaving behind a legacy that continues to inspire and awe those who venture to experience these masterpieces firsthand. As you explore these diverse destinations, you'll find yourself immersed in the beauty, innovation, and boundless creativity that have shaped the Mediterranean's architectural tapestry.

Culinary Delights

The Mediterranean is not only renowned for its breathtaking landscapes and historical marvels but also for its rich and diverse culinary heritage. From the savory bites of Greek mezze to the tantalizing array of tapas in Catalonia, the region offers a gastronomic journey that delights the senses and unveils the essence of its cultures.

Greek Mezze: An Array of Flavors

When it comes to indulging in Greek cuisine, the concept of 'mezze' takes center stage. Mezze, derived from the Persian word "mazze" which means taste or snack, is a style of dining that involves sharing an assortment of small dishes. It's not just a meal but an experience that encourages camaraderie and celebration.

Greek mezze is a reflection of the country's agricultural abundance and the Mediterranean's bounty. It's a showcase of fresh ingredients, bold flavors, and a harmonious blend of influences from ancient Greek, Ottoman, and Middle Eastern cuisines. Mezze spreads are often enjoyed as a prelude to the main meal, and they encompass a spectrum of tastes, textures, and aromas.

On the mezze platter, you'll find:

1. Taramasalata: A creamy dip made from fish roe, olive oil, lemon juice, and bread, offering a delightful balance of brininess and acidity.

2. Hummus: Though originating from the Middle East, hummus is a staple on Greek mezze platters. It's a smooth and velvety dip made from chickpeas, tahini, lemon, and garlic, usually drizzled with olive oil.

3. Dolmades: Grape leaves stuffed with a mixture of rice, herbs, and sometimes minced meat. These tender parcels are often served chilled and accompanied by yogurt sauce.

4. Spanakopita: A savory pastry filled with spinach, feta cheese, onions, and herbs, all enclosed in layers of flaky phyllo dough.

5. Kalamata Olives: Dark, wrinkled olives that are bursting with intense flavor. They can be served plain or marinated with herbs and citrus.

6. Feta Cheese: A quintessential ingredient in Greek cuisine, feta cheese is often crumbled over salads or served as a standalone dish.

7. Melitzanosalata: A dip made from roasted eggplant, garlic, olive oil, and herbs, offering a smoky and rich flavor.

8. Keftedes: Greek meatballs made from a mixture of ground meat (usually beef or lamb), herbs, and spices, often served with tzatziki sauce.

9. Fava: A creamy dip made from yellow split peas, typically seasoned with olive oil, lemon juice, and herbs.

10. Souvlaki: Skewers of grilled and marinated meat, often served with pita bread and garnished with vegetables and sauces.

11. Octopus Salad: Tender pieces of octopus marinated with olive oil, lemon, and herbs, creating a refreshing and tangy salad.

The Taste of Catalonia: Tapas and More

Catalonia, nestled in the northeastern corner of Spain, boasts its own culinary treasures with a focus on tapas, a concept that has transcended regional boundaries and captured the hearts of food enthusiasts worldwide. Tapas are small, flavorful dishes that can be enjoyed individually or combined to form a complete meal. These offerings are ideal for sharing, promoting a convivial atmosphere where friends and family come together.

Catalan tapas are characterized by their creativity, using a diverse range of ingredients that showcase the region's agricultural abundance and coastal proximity. Whether you're strolling through the vibrant streets of Barcelona or relaxing in a quaint seaside village, you'll encounter an enticing variety of tapas that highlight both tradition and innovation.

Some popular Catalan tapas include:

1. Patatas Bravas: Crispy potato cubes served with a spicy tomato-based sauce and creamy aioli. This dish perfectly balances heat and creaminess.

2. Croquettes: Fried rolls filled with ingredients like ham, cheese, or seafood. They have a crispy exterior and a creamy interior.

3. Pan con Tomate: A simple yet flavorful dish consisting of toasted bread rubbed with ripe tomatoes and drizzled with olive oil.

4. Pimientos de Padrón: Small green peppers blistered and seasoned with sea salt. While most are mild, occasionally, you'll find a spicy surprise.

5. Escalivada: Roasted vegetables, typically red bell peppers and eggplant, marinated in olive oil and garlic. It's a delightful medley of smoky flavors.

6. Butifarra: A Catalan sausage made from ground pork and spices, often served grilled or alongside other tapas.

7. Seafood Delights: Given Catalonia's coastal location, seafood tapas are a highlight. Grilled squid, marinated

anchovies, and shrimp dishes showcase the region's maritime influence.

8. Escudella i carn d'olla: A hearty Catalan stew made with various meats, vegetables, and legumes, often served during festive occasions.

9. Calçots: Grilled spring onions that are a regional delicacy, usually served with a romesco sauce made from almonds and red peppers.

10. Crema Catalana: A classic Catalan dessert similar to crème brûlée, featuring a creamy custard base topped with a layer of caramelized sugar.

11. Esqueixada: A refreshing salad made with salted cod, tomatoes, onions, olives, and peppers, drizzled with olive oil and vinegar.

12. Cava: While not a dish, Cava is a sparkling wine produced in Catalonia, often enjoyed as an accompaniment to meals and celebrations.

13. Canelons: Catalan-style cannelloni, typically filled with a mixture of meat or mushrooms and covered in creamy béchamel sauce.

14. Coca: A type of savory pastry topped with various ingredients like vegetables, meat, or fish, similar to a pizza but with a unique Catalan twist.

15. Perol: A seafood dish often served along the Costa Brava, featuring a medley of fresh seafood, rice, saffron, and other aromatic spices.

In Catalonia, tapas are not just about the food; they embody the spirit of sharing and socializing. It's common for locals and visitors alike to hop from one tapas bar to another, enjoying a diverse array of flavors and experiences along the way.

In conclusion, the culinary offerings of the Mediterranean region are a reflection of its history, culture, and geography. Greek mezze and Catalan tapas both exemplify the essence of Mediterranean dining – a celebration of community, fresh ingredients, and the joy of savoring every bite. Whether you're seated by the azure waters of the Aegean Sea or nestled in a bustling Spanish square, these culinary delights promise an unforgettable journey for the palate.

Chapter 3: Navigating the Mediterranean - Practical Travel Tips
Visa and Travel Documentation

Navigating Visa Requirements for Different Mediterranean Countries

As you embark on your Mediterranean adventure, one crucial aspect to consider is the visa and travel documentation required for the various countries you'll be visiting. The Mediterranean region comprises a diverse array of nations, each with its own set of entry requirements, making it essential to plan ahead to ensure a smooth and hassle-free journey.

Understanding Visa Types and Requirements in the Mediterranean Region

When embarking on a journey to the captivating Mediterranean region, one of the foremost aspects to consider is the intricate world of visa requirements. The Mediterranean is a tapestry of diverse countries, each with its own set of entry regulations, making it imperative to unravel the intricacies before setting foot on its sun-soaked shores.

Variability of Visa Requirements:
Visa regulations can vary significantly based on factors such as your nationality, the country you're entering, and the purpose of your visit. This spectrum of diversity is particularly evident within the Mediterranean region, which encompasses both Schengen Area countries and non-Schengen countries, each with its distinct entry procedures.

Schengen Area Countries: Seamless Travel Within Borders

The Schengen Area represents a collaborative arrangement among European countries that have abolished internal border controls. This group includes Mediterranean nations like France, Italy, Spain, and Greece. For travelers intending to explore the treasures of these Schengen countries, the Schengen Visa can be a passport to unrestricted travel within this zone for a predetermined period.

Schengen Visa Privileges:
The Schengen Visa offers the remarkable benefit of unrestricted travel across participating countries. This means that with a single visa, you can move freely between member countries without the need for additional documentation at internal borders. Whether you're strolling through the charming streets of Paris or basking on the beaches of Santorini, the Schengen Visa ensures a seamless travel experience.

Application Process:
Securing a Schengen Visa involves adhering to the specific requirements of the country you intend to visit first or spend the most time in. The application process typically involves providing essential documents such as a valid passport, a well-defined travel itinerary, proof of accommodation reservations, travel insurance coverage, and evidence of financial sufficiency to support your stay.

Non-Schengen Countries: A Spectrum of Entry Regulations

Beyond the Schengen Area, the Mediterranean region hosts countries with their own unique visa regulations. This includes destinations like Turkey and Morocco, each offering a distinctive set of entry requirements.

Diverse Entry Scenarios:
For travelers venturing into non-Schengen countries, the panorama of entry regulations is diverse. Some countries may offer visa-free entry for short stays to certain nationalities, while others might require advance visas for almost all visitors. It's crucial to delve into the specific entry requirements of your intended destination to avoid any unexpected complications upon arrival.

Research and Preparedness: Key Considerations
Research is your most reliable ally when navigating the Mediterranean's complex visa landscape. Here are some essential points to consider:

- Nationality Matters: Different nationalities might have different visa privileges and requirements for various countries. Always ascertain the specific visa conditions that apply to your citizenship.

- Purpose of Travel: The type of visa you need can vary based on the purpose of your visit – be it tourism, business, or other specific reasons.

- Entry and Exit Points: Depending on your travel route, you might encounter different entry points. Ensure you're informed about the visa requirements of each country you'll be entering.

- Advance Planning: Visa application processes can take time. Initiating the process well in advance of your intended travel dates can help prevent any last-minute challenges.

Packing Right for Varied Climates

Essentials for Sunny Beaches and Cooler Mountain Regions

One of the most enchanting aspects of a Mediterranean journey is its diverse range of climates. From the sun-drenched beaches of the Greek islands to the refreshing mountain air of the Pyrenees, the Mediterranean region presents travelers with a remarkable variety of environments to explore. As you embark on your Mediterranean adventure, packing smartly becomes essential to ensure your comfort and enjoyment throughout the trip.

Packing for Sunny Beaches: The Basics

When planning for beach destinations along the Mediterranean, it's all about embracing the sun, sand, and sea. Here's a list of essentials to ensure you're well-prepared for your beachfront experiences:

1. Swimwear: Pack a variety of swimsuits to suit different beach activities, whether you're lounging, swimming, or trying water sports.

2. Sun Protection: Bring along a wide-brimmed hat, sunglasses with UV protection, and a high SPF sunscreen to shield yourself from the intense Mediterranean sun.

3. Light Clothing: Opt for light and breathable clothing like cotton shirts, shorts, dresses, and sarongs to stay cool during the day.

4. Sandals and Flip-Flops: Comfortable footwear is a must for beach outings. Sandals and flip-flops are perfect for strolls on the shore.

5. Beach Bag: Carry a spacious beach bag to hold your essentials, such as sunscreen, water bottle, towel, and a good book.

6. Snorkeling Gear: If you're keen on exploring underwater wonders, consider bringing your own snorkeling gear for a more personal experience.

Packing for Cooler Mountain Regions: Staying Cozy and Stylish

As you venture into the cooler mountain regions surrounding the Mediterranean, packing for colder temperatures while maintaining style and comfort becomes paramount. Here's a checklist to ensure you're ready for the higher altitudes:

1. Layering Clothes: Pack versatile clothing that can be layered to adapt to changing temperatures. Long-sleeve shirts, sweaters, and a light jacket are great options.

2. Warm Accessories: Don't forget to bring gloves, a scarf, and a beanie to keep yourself warm while exploring mountain trails.

3. Sturdy Footwear: Comfortable and supportive hiking boots are a necessity if you plan to explore mountainous terrains. Additionally, pack a pair of comfortable sneakers for casual walks.

4. Rain Gear: Mountain weather can be unpredictable, so packing a compact rain jacket or a foldable umbrella is a wise choice.

5. Exploration Gear: If you're planning to hike or engage in outdoor activities, consider packing a daypack to carry essentials like water, snacks, a first-aid kit, and a map.

6. Casual and Dressy Attire: Even in cooler regions, you might want to explore local towns and dine at charming restaurants. Pack a few smart-casual outfits for such occasions.

7. Camera Equipment: The picturesque landscapes of mountain regions are perfect for photography enthusiasts. Bring along your camera, extra batteries, and memory cards.

Packing Pro Tips for Both Climates

- Travel Adapter: Remember to pack a travel adapter to charge your devices, as the plug configurations might differ from what you're used to.

- Reusable Water Bottle: Staying hydrated is important in all climates. A reusable water bottle helps you cut down on plastic waste and ensures you have water on hand at all times.

- First-Aid Kit: Prepare a small first-aid kit with essentials like bandages, pain relievers, and any prescription medications you might need.

- Local Attire Awareness: Research the local customs and dress codes of the regions you're visiting. This will help you pack appropriately and show respect for the local culture.

- Travel Insurance: Regardless of the climate, having comprehensive travel insurance is a prudent step to take. It provides coverage for unexpected events that could disrupt your trip.

Packing for varied climates along the Mediterranean requires a mix of practicality and style. By tailoring your packing list to the specific destinations and activities you have in mind, you'll be well-prepared to make the most of your Mediterranean adventure, whether you're basking on a sun-soaked beach or hiking through mountainous landscapes.

Transportation Options

Exploring Ferries, Trains, and Buses for Seamless Travel

Navigating the picturesque Mediterranean region is not only about the destinations you visit, but also the journeys that take you there. With its diverse landscapes and scattered archipelagos, the Mediterranean offers a variety of transportation options that provide not only practicality but also a chance to immerse yourself in the local way of life. From ferries that connect islands to trains that traverse historical routes and buses that wind through charming villages, the modes of transport in this region can truly enhance your travel experience.

Ferries: Connecting Islands and Coastal Gems

The Mediterranean Sea, with its sparkling azure waters and diverse archipelagos, beckons travelers to embark on a journey of discovery. Among the many transportation options available, ferries stand out as a magical conduit between mainland cities and the enchanting islands that pepper the horizon. These vessels are not just means of transportation; they are gateways to the allure and authenticity of Mediterranean island life.

Connecting Gems in the Sea: Island-to-Island and Mainland Links

Ferries play an essential role in knitting together the fabric of the Mediterranean's coastal communities. Imagine standing at the edge of a bustling harbor, watching as a ferry departs for a nearby island. The sight evokes a sense of adventure, as if you're about to set sail on a voyage reminiscent of explorers from eras past.

The connections ferries provide are not just utilitarian; they embody the Mediterranean's spirit of unity in diversity. Islands that were once remote and isolated are now intricately linked to the mainland and to each other, fostering cultural exchange and the sharing of traditions. These vessels are lifelines that carry people, goods, and stories across the vast blue expanse.

A Voyage of Enchantment: Sailing the Azure Waters

Sailing on a ferry through the Mediterranean Sea is a captivating experience that awakens the senses. The gentle rock of the boat, the soothing sound of waves lapping against the hull, and the salty breeze that carries the essence of the sea – all contribute to a symphony of sensations that create lasting memories.

Imagine embarking on a ferry from Naples, Italy, destined for the breathtaking Isle of Capri. As the ferry glides away from the mainland, the Tyrrhenian Sea stretches out in all directions, its deep blue hues merging seamlessly with the sky. The anticipation of reaching the island grows with each passing minute, as you glimpse the distant cliffs and vibrant harbors that mark its presence.

Island Dreams: A Glimpse of Unique Charms

Each Mediterranean island is a microcosm of culture, history, and natural beauty. The ferry journey itself offers tantalizing glimpses of what's to come. In Greece, ferries whisk travelers between the Cyclades Islands, providing an opportunity to hop from one idyllic paradise to another.

Imagine hopping on a ferry in Mykonos, where the vibrant energy of the island's beaches and nightlife lingers in the air. After a leisurely cruise, you step onto the shores of Santorini, a place of romance and captivating sunsets. The ferry becomes a magical time machine, transporting you from the liveliness of Mykonos to the romantic tranquility of Santorini in mere hours.

The Voyage as a Destination

In the Mediterranean, the journey is as much a part of the experience as the destination itself. Ferries, with their ability to seamlessly connect mainland cities and remote islands, offer a unique perspective on the region's beauty, culture, and interconnectedness. The azure waters of the Mediterranean hold more than just a physical expanse; they hold the promise of adventure, the enchantment of discovery, and the warmth of shared experiences.

So, as you stand at the ferry terminal, gazing out at the horizon, remember that the journey you're about to embark upon is not merely a means to an end. It's an integral part of the story, a chapter that weaves together the tapestry of your Mediterranean adventure.

Trains: A Window into History and Culture

For travelers with a penchant for slow exploration and a desire to intimately connect with the history and cultures of the Mediterranean, there's a realm of enchantment waiting aboard its scenic train routes. These journeys are more than mere transportation; they're immersive experiences that unveil the region's soul through captivating landscapes and glimpses into local life.

While the Mediterranean is renowned for its sun-soaked beaches and historical treasures, its train journeys often remain a hidden gem, offering a unique perspective on its diverse tapestry.

A Symphony of Nature: The Flam Railway, Norway

Though not directly nestled in the Mediterranean, the Flam Railway in Norway serves as an exemplary ode to the beauty of train travel in Europe. As one of the world's most scenic train rides, it offers an insight into the allure that awaits travelers on Mediterranean rail routes.

Amidst the backdrop of the Norwegian fjords, the Flam Railway winds through dramatic landscapes that leave passengers awestruck. Cascading waterfalls, mirror-like lakes, and snow-capped peaks compose a symphony of nature's beauty. The journey becomes an immersive experience, where the rhythmic clatter of the train melds with the whispering winds and rushing waters. It's a reminder that a train ride can be a destination in itself, a meditative sojourn that allows passengers to absorb the world around them.

Mediterranean Romance: The Barcelona to Valencia Route, Spain

Within the Mediterranean's embrace, the allure of scenic train journeys takes on a unique character, blending history, culture, and landscapes in perfect harmony. The Barcelona to Valencia route in Spain is a testament to this. This journey isn't just about moving from one city to another; it's a passage through the heart of Spain's countryside.

As the train departs Barcelona's bustling streets, it ventures into the tranquil landscapes of Catalonia. Olive groves stretch to the horizon, their silvery leaves shimmering in the sun. Vineyards come into view, with neat rows of grapevines painted against the backdrop of rolling hills. Along the way, medieval towns such as Tarragona and Castellón evoke the romance of bygone eras, their historic architecture bearing witness to centuries of stories.

A Tapestry of Culture and History

What sets these train journeys apart is the seamless blending of the natural and the cultural. The Mediterranean, with its history steeped in trade, conquest, and coexistence, unravels like a living tapestry from the window of a train. The stone villages perched on hillsides tell tales of resilience, while the terraced fields narrate the triumph of human effort over challenging landscapes.

These journeys invite contemplation. Passengers find themselves contemplating the layers of history that have shaped the region, from the Roman ruins dotting the Italian coast to the Moorish influences seen in Andalusian architecture. The train becomes a moving time machine, whisking travelers through epochs while inviting them to savor the present moment.

In a world where speed often defines travel, the Mediterranean's scenic train journeys offer a refreshing alternative. They remind us that the journey is as important as the destination, that a train ride can be an immersive experience that deepens our connection with the places we traverse. Whether it's the flamboyant colors of Norway's fjords or the earthy hues of Spain's countryside, these journeys unveil the heart and soul of the Mediterranean in ways that are both captivating and profound.

Buses: Winding Through Authentic Villages

Amid the enchanting Mediterranean region, where every corner holds a story and every alley whispers tales of centuries gone by, buses emerge as the unsung heroes of transportation. Far beyond being mere modes of getting from one place to another, buses become the conduits that lead intrepid travelers to the heart of authenticity, revealing places and experiences that lie off the well-trodden path.

Off the Beaten Path: Unveiling Hidden Treasures

In a world where tourist attractions often take center stage, buses provide a different kind of journey – one that lets you uncover hidden gems. The Mediterranean's charm lies not only in its renowned cities but also in its tucked-away villages and lesser-known towns that resonate with history and culture. Buses weave their way through these narrow alleys and winding streets, taking you to places that larger vehicles could never traverse.

Picture this: you're journeying through the rugged, awe-inspiring landscapes of the Amalfi Coast in Italy. Here, buses transform into agile companions, deftly navigating the precarious hairpin bends that hug the cliffsides. As you peer out of the window, the coastline stretches beneath you, revealing a panorama that words can scarcely capture. This bus ride isn't just a means of transport; it's an adventure etched with breathtaking vistas and heart-pounding thrills.

Connecting with Local Life: A Glimpse into Authenticity

Buses offer more than just a ride – they grant you an intimate view into the daily lives of the people who call the Mediterranean home. In a region where culture and tradition run deep, the daily commute becomes a part of the local tapestry. Buses serve as vessels of connection, ferrying residents to markets, workplaces, and celebrations, allowing you to become a temporary participant in this cultural dance.

Imagine yourself in the serene countryside of Provence, France. Here, buses meander through fields of fragrant lavender and verdant vineyards. As the bus ambles along, you're surrounded by the soft hues and heady scents that define the Provençal landscape. The destination? Charming villages like Gordes and Roussillon – oases of tranquility and authenticity. Stepping off the bus, you're greeted by cobblestone streets, rustic facades, and the warm smiles of locals. The Provençal atmosphere envelopes you, and you're not just a traveler passing through; you're an observer of life, a participant in a narrative that unfolds with every footstep.

The Essence of Discovery

Buses in the Mediterranean are more than metal and wheels; they're gateways to discovery. They embody the spirit of exploration, carrying you beyond the predictable and scripted, unveiling the essence of the region. They allow you to taste the salt in the air as you breeze through coastal towns, to feel the pulse of tradition as you traverse ancient pathways, and to experience the camaraderie of locals as you share a brief moment of shared space.

So, as you plan your Mediterranean adventure, consider the stories that buses can unveil. Beyond schedules and routes, they offer an opportunity to step into the rhythm of life, to journey not just through geography but through the fabric of culture and history. With each bus ride, you're not merely a spectator; you're an active participant in a narrative that carries the essence of the Mediterranean's soul.

Seamless Integration for Unforgettable Journeys

What makes transportation in the Mediterranean truly remarkable is how seamlessly these modes of travel integrate with the overall experience. Ferries, trains, and buses aren't just about getting from one point to another; they're about feeling the rhythm of a place, witnessing its everyday life, and connecting with its history and people.

Whether you're island hopping in Croatia, exploring the historical sites of Rome, or wandering the streets of Istanbul, the Mediterranean's transportation options weave an intricate tapestry of experiences. They offer a chance to slow down, soak in the surroundings, and engage with the region's authenticity. So, as you plan your Mediterranean adventure, consider the journey itself as an integral part of the whole experience – a chance to discover the heart and soul of this captivating region from a unique perspective.

Chapter 4: Basking in Mediterranean Sun - Outdoor Activities

The Mediterranean's inviting climate and pristine waters provide an ideal setting for a myriad of outdoor activities that cater to both relaxation seekers and adventure enthusiasts. In this chapter, we delve into the world of sun-soaked beaches and exhilarating water sports, exploring two captivating experiences that define the region's allure.

Beach Escapes and Water Sports

Snorkeling in Cyprus' Blue Lagoon

Nestled on the picturesque coastline of Cyprus, the Blue Lagoon is a haven for snorkelers and underwater enthusiasts. This serene, turquoise-hued cove boasts crystal-clear waters that allow for unparalleled visibility into the underwater world. As you don your snorkeling gear and dip into the gentle embrace of the lagoon, you'll be greeted by a kaleidoscope of marine life. Schools of vibrant fish flit around the coral formations, creating a mesmerizing display of colors. Keep an eye out for the charming seahorses that sometimes make appearances, seemingly posing for the delighted snorkelers.

The Blue Lagoon's calm waters make it an ideal spot for beginners and families looking to introduce themselves to the wonders of snorkeling. The absence of strong currents and waves ensures a safe and enjoyable experience for all ages. If you're feeling more adventurous, you can explore the rocky crevices and hidden nooks that are home to curious crustaceans and tiny fish seeking refuge. The experience of floating above this thriving underwater ecosystem is nothing short of enchanting, offering a sense of serenity and connection with nature that is truly unparalleled.

Windsurfing Adventures off the Sicilian Coast

For those seeking a more invigorating experience, the windswept coasts of Sicily offer the perfect backdrop for windsurfing aficionados. With its steady sea breezes and impressive waves, the Mediterranean Sea becomes your playground as you harness the power of the wind to glide across the water's surface with finesse and grace.

The northwestern coast of Sicily, particularly around the popular town of Trapani, is a windsurfing paradise. The reliable "Mistral" winds, blowing in from the northwest, create ideal conditions for both beginners and experienced windsurfers. Schools and rental shops dot the coastline, ready to provide you with the necessary equipment and instruction to get you started.

As you stand on your board and feel the wind filling your sail, you'll experience a rush of adrenaline unlike any other. The sensation of gliding across the water, the spray of saltwater on your skin, and the stunning coastal views create a truly immersive experience. For those looking to take their skills to the next level, Trapani hosts windsurfing clinics and events that attract enthusiasts from around the world, fostering a vibrant community of like-minded adventurers.

Exploring Sea Caves in Malta's Azure Waters

In the heart of the Mediterranean lies the archipelago of Malta, a haven for adventurous souls seeking a truly unique aquatic experience. The island's rocky coastline is adorned with hidden treasures in the form of mesmerizing sea caves, waiting to be explored by intrepid travelers. Picture yourself gliding atop the serene azure waters on a kayak or a paddleboard, a gentle breeze brushing against your skin as you navigate the labyrinth of caves that have been sculpted by the ceaseless caress of the sea.

As you venture deeper into these mysterious caverns, you'll find yourself immersed in a world of wonder. The interplay of sunlight filtering through openings in the rocky ceiling casts enchanting patterns of light and shadow on the water's surface, creating an ethereal atmosphere that's nothing short of captivating. The hushed echoes of lapping waves within the caves add to the sense of tranquility, providing a unique opportunity for introspection and connection with the natural world.

The cool embrace of the caves is a welcome relief from the warm Mediterranean sun, offering a reprieve from the outside world and allowing you to be fully present in the moment. With every stroke of your paddle, you'll uncover hidden nooks and crannies, each with its own story to tell. The sea caves of Malta not only showcase the astonishing power of nature's artistry but also provide a sanctuary for those seeking solace and an intimate connection with the sea.

Kiteboarding on the Costa del Sol

The Costa del Sol, located along the sun-drenched shores of southern Spain, is renowned for its golden beaches and vibrant coastal towns. However, this Mediterranean gem is also a haven for adrenaline junkies seeking an exhilarating rush on the waves. Kiteboarding, a thrilling water sport that combines elements of surfing, wakeboarding, and paragliding, has found a perfect home on the shores of the Costa del Sol.

Imagine standing on the shore, the wind tugging at your kite as you prepare to launch into an aquatic adventure. With a powerful gust, you're off, skimming across the water's surface with a sense of freedom that's unparalleled. The wind becomes your ally as you manipulate the kite's movement, propelling yourself across the waves and into the air for heart-stopping jumps and spins that defy gravity.

For beginners, the Costa del Sol offers a range of kiteboarding schools staffed by experienced instructors who are passionate about sharing their love for the sport. They'll guide you through the basics of controlling the kite, maintaining balance on the board, and riding the waves. Even seasoned kiteboarders will find themselves challenged by the varying wind conditions and the excitement of mastering new tricks against the backdrop of the Mediterranean's endless horizon.

Cliff Diving in the Calanques of Provence

Nestled along the rugged coastline of Provence in France, the Calanques offer an entirely different way to experience the Mediterranean's allure – through the adrenaline-pumping adventure of cliff diving. These steep-sided inlets are characterized by their dramatic beauty and deep turquoise waters, creating a picturesque setting for those seeking an invigorating thrill.

Standing at the edge of a towering cliff, you'll gaze out at the expansive sea below, its vibrant hues beckoning you to take the plunge. The breeze ruffles your hair as your heart races in anticipation. As you step off the edge, the rush of wind fills your ears, and a moment later, you're immersed in the cool embrace of the sea. The impact is exhilarating, the experience both humbling and electrifying.

The Calanques' cliffs vary in height, offering options for both seasoned cliff divers and those new to the experience. For the daring, there are higher jumps that provide a heart-pounding adrenaline rush, while lower jumps offer a chance to ease into the adventure. Regardless of the height you choose, the turquoise waters below invite you to connect with the untamed spirit of the Mediterranean in a way that's both exhilarating and deeply fulfilling.

Sailing the Adriatic: Croatian Coastline Exploration

Embarking on a sailing journey along the Croatian coastline is akin to stepping into a maritime wonderland where time seems to slow down and the boundaries between history and nature blur. The Adriatic Sea, with its rich history and diverse geography, becomes your canvas as you set sail amidst the mosaic of over a thousand islands, islets, and reefs that make up Croatia's picturesque archipelago. This labyrinthine seascape offers sailors an unparalleled playground, where every corner reveals a new discovery.

As your sailboat glides through the gentle waves, you'll find yourself surrounded by breathtaking vistas at every turn. The Croatian coastline is a symphony of contrasts – from the ancient walled city of Dubrovnik, with its terracotta roofs and imposing fortress walls, to the untouched beauty of the Elafiti Islands, where nature's hand has sculpted untouched landscapes.

Island-hopping takes on new dimensions here. Each island tells its own story – from the vibrant energy of Hvar, with its bustling harbor and vibrant nightlife, to the serene tranquility of Vis, where time seems to stand still. Drop anchor in secluded bays and hidden coves, where the azure waters invite you to take a refreshing dip or snorkel in underwater realms teeming with life.

But sailing the Croatian Adriatic isn't just about the destinations; it's about the journey itself. As you navigate through these storied waters, you'll feel the weight of history whispering through the winds. Sail past ancient trade routes that once connected empires and pause to explore fishing villages that have retained their maritime traditions for generations.

Kayaking the Calanques: A Provencal Adventure

Imagine skimming over the surface of the Mediterranean, your kayak slicing through the cerulean waters, as the rugged limestone cliffs of the Calanques rise majestically around you. This is a Provencal adventure that immerses you in the untamed beauty of the French coast in a way that few experiences can match.

As you paddle through the hidden inlets and fjords of the Calanques National Park, you'll experience nature's grandeur in its purest form. The towering cliffs create a dramatic backdrop, their hues shifting with the changing sunlight. The rhythmic lapping of waves against the rock formations and the occasional cry of seabirds become your soundtrack, creating a serene symphony that soothes the senses.

These waters reveal hidden secrets, and as you kayak further into the heart of the Calanques, you'll stumble upon secluded beaches accessible only by water. These tucked-away gems offer a space of solace and tranquility, inviting you to take a break, swim in the refreshing waters, and simply absorb the beauty around you.

Exploring Sea Caves in Sardinia

Sardinia, an exquisite jewel nestled within the embrace of the Mediterranean Sea, holds within its coastline a hidden world of wonder waiting to be explored. Beyond its famed beaches lies a secret realm of sea caves, each a portal to a realm of natural artistry and marine life. As you embark on this aquatic adventure, equipped with your snorkeling gear and a sense of curiosity, you step into an otherworldly domain where the boundaries between water and stone blur.

Venturing into these mysterious caverns is like entering a gallery of nature's most intricate designs. Sunlight, filtering through the underwater apertures, paints a mesmerizing tableau of ethereal hues. The gentle play of light and shadow illuminates the marine tapestry that has taken centuries to craft. Here, you become an observer in an undersea theater, where fish dart and dance among the coral formations, and algae sway like aquatic ballet dancers.

The sea caves of Sardinia hold a symphony of life, from the smallest iridescent fish to the grandeur of occasional sea turtles gliding through their aquatic sanctuaries. You're not just snorkeling; you're a participant in an ecosystem, a silent witness to the interactions that unfold in the quiet corners of these submerged cathedrals.

As you glide through the calm waters within these caves, the world outside seems to melt away, leaving you with a heightened sense of connection to the ocean's mysteries. Intricate rock formations, shaped by the ceaseless embrace of the waves, bear witness to the passage of time. The interplay of light and shadow creates an ever-changing tapestry, an eternal dance upon the cave walls that paints your journey with a touch of the ethereal.

Kitesurfing along the Algarve Coast

The Algarve, Portugal's southern coastal gem, is a region where the union of wind and waves has crafted an arena of boundless excitement – a haven for kitesurfing aficionados. Here, the expansive coastline stretches out like a canvas, painted with golden beaches and dramatic cliffs, where the wind is your ally and the waves your playground.

In the world of kitesurfing, you're more than a spectator; you're a performer riding nature's forces. As you stand on the shore, the kite tugging at your grasp, you feel the elemental power waiting to lift you off the water's surface. And then, with the wind as your engine, you're airborne. The thrill is palpable as you glide across the water's expanse, defying gravity with each jump and maneuver.

The Algarve's diverse beaches offer experiences for all levels, whether you're a seasoned kitesurfer craving the adrenaline of challenging waves or a newcomer eager to learn the art of harnessing the wind. Kitesurfing schools dot the coast, staffed by experts ready to guide you through the exhilarating learning curve.

Yet, it's not just about the sport; it's about the symphony of sensations that come with it. The spray of saltwater, the feel of the wind's embrace, and the rush of excitement as you execute a trick – all combine to create an experience that resonates with the dynamic energy of the Algarve.

Trails of the Cinque Terre

Nestled like precious gems along the rugged Italian Riviera, the Cinque Terre's five enchanting villages are connected not only by their picturesque charm but also by a network of trails that unveil a treasure trove of nature's beauty. As you set foot on these trails, you embark on a journey that traverses not only land but also time, immersing you in an ancient landscape where human craftsmanship harmonizes with nature's splendor.

The paths that wind through the Cinque Terre are a testament to the human spirit's harmonious coexistence with the land. As you hike along these routes, you're greeted by breathtaking vistas of the turquoise waters below and the terraced hillsides that cradle the villages. The intoxicating scent of olive groves and vineyards mingles with the salty breeze, creating a sensory symphony that complements the visual feast.

Each step carries you from one charming village to the next, revealing unique perspectives of the Mediterranean's azure embrace. The narrow streets of these villages beckon, offering glimpses into local life and culture. The aromas of freshly caught seafood waft from local trattorias, inviting you to savor the flavors of the sea and the land.

The Cinque Terre trails are not just about hiking; they're about forging a connection with the land and the people who call it home. They tell stories of generations who have walked these paths, tended the vineyards, and sculpted the terraces that define the landscape. In each step, you become a part of this legacy, a participant in the dialogue between humanity and nature that has shaped the Cinque Terre for centuries.

Cycling the Peloponnese Peninsula: Greece's Scenic Routes

For those who prefer the firm ground beneath their feet, cycling through Greece's Peloponnese Peninsula is a journey that intertwines history, culture, and natural splendor. This diverse landscape presents a dynamic canvas for your exploration – from winding coastal roads that hug the azure shoreline to lush valleys framed by ancient olive groves and dramatic mountain passes that offer panoramic views of the sparkling Mediterranean Sea.

Pedaling through the Peloponnese is a journey through time itself. Ancient ruins stand as testament to the region's storied past, and as you cycle past these remnants of antiquity, you can almost hear the echoes of civilizations that have shaped the land. Olive groves and vineyards offer a glimpse into the agricultural heritage that sustains local communities, while charming villages seemingly frozen in time invite you to pause, interact with locals, and savor the warmth of Greek hospitality.

The climax of your journey comes as you ascend the slopes of Mount Taygetos, a challenging feat that rewards you with sweeping vistas that extend from the rugged mountains to the glistening sea. The descent into seaside towns is a delight, and the promise of fresh seafood and a hearty Greek meal serves as a beacon of welcome after your cycling triumphs.

In essence, cycling the Peloponnese isn't just a physical adventure; it's an immersion into the heart of Greece's captivating heritage. Each pedal stroke carries you further into a world where landscapes whisper tales of the past and where the spirit of exploration takes you on a journey of discovery.

Whether you're content to explore the underwater wonders of Cyprus' Blue Lagoon or seek the thrill of windsurfing off the Sicilian coast, the Mediterranean's outdoor offerings cater to a wide range of interests and preferences. These activities are a testament to the region's ability to captivate and exhilarate travelers, creating memories that are as vibrant as the landscapes themselves. The Mediterranean's waters beckon, inviting you to discover the magic that lies beneath the surface and to ride the winds that have shaped its shores for centuries. So, don your snorkel or embrace the windsurfing rig, and let the Mediterranean's natural beauty envelop you in an unforgettable embrace of sun and sea.

Hiking and Nature Exploration

The Mediterranean region is not only renowned for its stunning beaches and rich history, but it also offers an array of breathtaking landscapes that are a paradise for outdoor enthusiasts. From the rugged terrains of Turkey to the lush trails of Corsica, hiking in the Mediterranean provides a unique opportunity to connect with nature while immersing oneself in the region's natural beauty.

Hiking the Samaria Gorge in Crete, Greece

For those seeking a remarkable natural adventure, the Samaria Gorge in Crete beckons with its dramatic landscapes and challenging terrain. Known as one of Europe's longest gorges, this hike takes you through a diverse ecosystem, from dense pine forests to arid rocky expanses.

The trail begins at the Omalos Plateau, where hikers descend into the gorge's depths, surrounded by towering cliffs that reach up to 1,000 meters high. The trail's narrow passages and uneven terrain add an element of excitement as you navigate through its twists and turns. Along the way, the refreshing waters of the River Tarraios offer a chance to cool off before the final stretch.

Reaching the village of Agia Roumeli at the end of the hike, hikers can reward themselves with a dip in the Mediterranean Sea and a taste of Cretan cuisine. The Samaria Gorge hike not only provides a physical challenge but also a memorable immersion into Crete's natural beauty.

Trekking the Lycian Way in Turkey

The Lycian Way, a long-distance hiking trail in Turkey, offers a captivating blend of history and natural beauty for those seeking an immersive outdoor adventure. Spanning approximately 540 kilometers along the country's southwestern coast, this trail winds through diverse landscapes, ancient ruins, and charming villages.

Starting in the coastal town of Fethiye, the Lycian Way leads hikers through fragrant pine forests, across rugged mountains, and along azure coastlines. The trail is peppered with historical sites that whisper tales of the Lycian civilization, such as the ghostly city of Patara and the striking rock-cut tombs of Myra.

One of the trail's most iconic sections is the ascent to Mount Olympos, which rewards trekkers with panoramic views of the Mediterranean Sea and surrounding landscapes. As the trail descends, it takes hikers to hidden gems like the idyllic beach of Cirali, where the pristine waters offer a refreshing respite after a day's journey.

The Lycian Way isn't just about physical exertion; it's also an opportunity to immerse oneself in Turkish culture. Hikers can interact with locals in quaint villages, savor traditional cuisine, and witness the rhythms of daily life. From sipping tea in cozy teahouses to sharing stories with fellow travelers in guesthouses, the trail fosters connections that enrich the journey.

Exploring Corsica's Scenic Trails

Corsica, an enchanting Mediterranean island belonging to France, boasts a diverse landscape that ranges from lush forests to rugged cliffs. Its network of hiking trails provides an escape into nature's wonders and a chance to discover the island's unique charm.

The Mare e Monti trail, translating to "Sea and Mountains," showcases Corsica's contrasting landscapes in one breathtaking journey. This trail traverses through serene forests, quaint villages, and alongside the glistening Mediterranean waters. Hikers can savor stunning sunsets as they walk along coastal paths, with the scent of wildflowers wafting through the air.

Venturing into the heart of Corsica, the GR20 trail challenges intrepid hikers with its demanding terrain. As one of Europe's most challenging long-distance trails, the GR20 offers a true test of endurance. The trail leads through jagged peaks, alpine meadows, and rustic refuges, offering an unforgettable experience for those seeking a profound connection with nature.

Corsica's landscape isn't just about mountains and coasts; it's also a haven for birdwatchers and nature enthusiasts. The Scandola Nature Reserve, a UNESCO World Heritage site, is a sanctuary for rare birds like the osprey and peregrine falcon. Hikers can witness these majestic creatures in their natural habitat while exploring this protected area.

The trails of Corsica also provide opportunities to delve into its rich history. Ruined fortresses, ancient churches, and picturesque hamlets dot the landscape, inviting hikers to journey back in time. Each step taken on these trails is a step into the past and a chance to connect with the island's cultural heritage.

Traversing the Alpes-Maritimes Trails in France

The Alpes-Maritimes region in southeastern France offers a treasure trove of hiking trails that wind through Alpine landscapes, charming villages, and historic sites. From the Mercantour National Park to the medieval town of Entrevaux, hikers can explore a diverse range of terrains and experiences.

The Vallée des Merveilles (Valley of Marvels) is a highlight, known for its ancient rock engravings that date back thousands of years. The trails here take hikers through alpine meadows, glacial lakes, and awe-inspiring vistas of the surrounding peaks.

In addition to natural beauty, the Alpes-Maritimes region also offers cultural immersion, with trails passing through quaint villages where you can sample local cheeses, wines, and pastries. The variety of trails ensures that hikers of all skill levels can find a suitable path to explore this enchanting corner of France.

Discovering the Troodos Mountains Trails in Cyprus

Cyprus, known for its stunning coastline, also offers captivating mountain landscapes waiting to be explored. The Troodos Mountains are a hiker's paradise, featuring dense forests, picturesque villages, and charming Byzantine churches.

The Caledonia Waterfall Trail is a popular choice, leading hikers to the highest waterfall on the island. The trail meanders through lush vegetation, offering glimpses of unique flora and fauna. As you approach the waterfall, the sound of rushing water and the cool mist create a refreshing atmosphere.

The Troodos Mountains also hold cultural treasures, including the painted churches of the region. These UNESCO-listed churches feature intricate frescoes that provide insights into Cyprus' rich history and religious traditions. Exploring the Troodos Mountains is a journey through nature and culture that offers a different perspective on the Mediterranean island.

Montenegro's Durmitor National Park

Nestled within the heart of the Balkans, Montenegro's Durmitor National Park stands as a pristine wilderness awaiting the discovery of intrepid hikers and nature enthusiasts. This hidden gem, bestowed with the honor of being a UNESCO World Heritage site, boasts an enchanting tapestry of rugged mountains, serene glacial lakes, and dense, untouched forests that beckon to the adventurous souls seeking solace in the great outdoors.

For hikers seeking a range of experiences, Durmitor National Park offers a myriad of trails tailored to varying skill levels. The park's crown jewel, the Black Lake Trail, is a picturesque journey that meanders around the glistening Black Lake. With every step, the lake mirrors the majesty of the towering peaks that encompass it, creating a tranquil reflection of nature's artistry.

For the more daring adventurers, the trails leading to Bobotov Kuk, the highest peak in the park, provide an exhilarating ascent that culminates in panoramic vistas that leave hikers in awe. From this lofty vantage point, the landscapes below unfold like a vibrant tapestry, revealing the intricate patterns of verdant valleys and alpine meadows that stretch into the distance.

As the sun sets beyond the peaks, the skies above Durmitor National Park transform into a canvas of stars, offering a celestial spectacle that few places can rival. Camping under these twinkling lights offers a chance to immerse oneself in the serenity of nature's embrace, fostering a deep connection to the wild beauty of Montenegro's heartland.

Amalfi Coast's Path of the Gods, Italy

Italy's Amalfi Coast is a paradise for travelers seeking both natural beauty and rich cultural experiences. With its charming towns clinging to cliffs above the azure waters of the Mediterranean Sea, the region captivates the imagination. Amidst this stunning landscape lies a hiking trail that lives up to its heavenly name – the "Sentiero degli Dei," or the Path of the Gods.

This hiking trail is a true gem, offering a moderate challenge that rewards hikers with breathtaking vistas that seem to transcend earthly boundaries. As you embark on the journey, the trail winds its way along the coastline, revealing awe-inspiring panoramas at every turn. The shimmering sea stretches as far as the eye can see, merging with the sky in a captivating dance of colors.

What makes the Path of the Gods truly special is its ability to immerse hikers in the essence of the Amalfi Coast. The trail meanders through terraced vineyards, where the scent of ripening grapes mingles with the salty sea breeze. Fragrant lemon groves line the path, their bright yellow fruits offering a sensory delight. Charming villages, seemingly suspended between heaven and earth, invite you to pause and embrace the local culture.

As you ascend higher, the drama of the coastline unfolds before you. The rugged cliffs plunge into the sea, creating a breathtaking backdrop against which the waves crash and play. These awe-inspiring views are an artist's dream and a reminder of the splendor of the natural world.

Reaching the summit, a sense of accomplishment merges with the sheer beauty that surrounds you. From this vantage point, you can trace the path you've taken and witness the journey of the sun as it paints the sky with hues of gold and pink during sunset. It's a moment of pure connection – with nature, with the history of the land, and with the sublime.

The Path of the Gods isn't just a hike; it's a pilgrimage through the heart of the Amalfi Coast. Each step is a testament to the region's allure, its ability to inspire wonder, and its power to leave an indelible mark on those who traverse its trails. So lace up your hiking boots, breathe in the salty air, and embark on a journey that promises not only panoramic views but also a profound connection with one of Italy's most stunning landscapes.

Monte Titano: Scaling the Heights of San Marino

Perched high on a hilltop in the heart of Italy lies the enclave of San Marino – a sovereign state surrounded by Italy. While its small size may belie its significance, this picturesque destination offers a unique hiking experience that showcases both natural beauty and historical intrigue.

The focal point of San Marino is Monte Titano, the highest peak in the region. Ascending its heights is an adventure that promises both physical challenge and spiritual reward. The well-marked trails guide you through a forested landscape, where the rustling leaves and the chorus of birds create a serene atmosphere. The climb is punctuated by glimpses of historic fortifications, testaments to the enclave's storied past.

As you ascend, the views expand, gradually revealing a panorama that stretches from the Apennine Mountains to the sparkling Adriatic Sea. The effort invested in the ascent is repaid tenfold by the sense of accomplishment and the profound connection with the land that only such endeavors can provide.

The summit of Monte Titano is a culmination of both physical and visual grandeur. As you stand atop this peak, you'll witness a breathtaking canvas that encompasses rolling hills, charming villages, and the vast expanse of the sea. It's a vantage point that allows you to contemplate the layers of history that have unfolded beneath your feet.

Scaling the heights of Monte Titano isn't just a hike; it's a journey through time, an exploration of a microcosm that represents the essence of San Marino. It's a testament to the resilience of a small nation, the allure of nature's beauty, and the power of human endeavor to conquer challenges both physical and metaphorical.

Coastal Trails of the French Riviera: Cap d'Antibes to Cap Ferrat

The French Riviera, synonymous with glamour and luxury, is also home to some of the most enchanting coastal trails in the Mediterranean. Amidst the glitz and glamour, these trails offer a chance to connect with nature, soaking in the region's innate beauty.

One of these trails stretches from Cap d'Antibes to Cap Ferrat, two iconic headlands that grace the coastline with their distinctive charm. The trail leads hikers along rugged cliffs, past hidden coves kissed by the turquoise waters, and offers glimpses of luxurious villas that dot the landscape. This enchanting hike strikes a balance between the lush Mediterranean vegetation and the spellbinding sea views that have inspired artists and writers for centuries.

As you set foot on the trail, you'll find yourself immersed in the soothing embrace of the coastal breeze. The scent of salt mingles with the fragrance of wildflowers, creating an olfactory symphony that is uniquely Mediterranean. The trail, lined with vibrant bougainvillaea and aromatic herbs, leads you on a journey of sensory delights.

The captivating views are a constant companion as you traverse the rugged terrain. Azure waters stretch to the horizon, changing hues under the caress of the sun. Secluded coves invite you to take a refreshing dip in the

Mediterranean's embrace, while the cliffs provide ample perches to pause and contemplate the beauty of the world around you.

This coastal hike is more than a physical adventure; it's a testament to the region's natural splendor. The trail encapsulates the essence of the French Riviera – a harmonious blend of opulent living and untamed landscapes. It's a reminder that amidst the sophistication, there lies a pristine world of unspoiled beauty, waiting to be explored.

Exploring Corsica's Scenic Trails

Corsica, often referred to as the "Island of Beauty," is a rugged gem nestled in the Mediterranean Sea. Its diverse landscapes, ranging from snow-capped mountains to pristine beaches, make it a haven for nature lovers and hikers. With a network of well-maintained trails, Corsica offers a range of options for hikers of all levels.

The GR20, known as one of the most challenging long-distance hikes in Europe, traverses the island diagonally from north to south. This demanding trail offers a thrilling adventure for experienced hikers, taking them through remote landscapes, mountain passes, and challenging terrain. Along the way, hikers can enjoy breathtaking vistas of lush valleys and sparkling blue waters.

For those seeking a more leisurely hiking experience, Corsica provides numerous shorter trails that allow explorers to immerse themselves in the island's natural beauty without the intensity of the GR20. The Calanques de Piana, a UNESCO World Heritage site, showcases impressive red rock formations and hidden coves accessible via well-marked trails.

Corsica's hiking trails also offer a chance to encounter its unique flora and fauna. The island is home to several endemic species, including the Corsican pine and mouflon sheep. Hikers may also spot birds of prey soaring overhead and the vibrant colors of wildflowers lining the trails during the spring and summer months.

As hikers traverse Corsica's landscapes, they have the opportunity to experience local culture and cuisine in charming villages along the way. Corsican cuisine, influenced by both French and Italian flavors, features fresh seafood, aromatic herbs, and artisanal cheeses that provide a delicious reward after a day on the trails.

In conclusion, hiking and nature exploration in the Mediterranean present an incredible blend of adventure, history, and natural beauty. Whether embarking on the ancient trails of the Lycian Way in Turkey or venturing into the diverse landscapes of Corsica, hikers are sure to be captivated by the region's stunning vistas, unique flora and fauna, and the sense of accomplishment that comes from conquering these trails.

Chapter 5: Immersing in Local Life - Accommodation and Interaction

Charming Boutique Stays

Experiencing Rustic Farmstays in the Mediterranean Countryside

When it comes to truly immersing yourself in the local life of the Mediterranean, your choice of accommodation can make all the difference. While luxury hotels and resorts certainly have their allure, there's something uniquely authentic about staying in charming boutique accommodations that allow you to connect intimately with the surrounding culture and environment. One such enchanting option that offers a genuine experience is the rustic farmstay, where you can escape the hustle and bustle of the city and embrace the serene rhythms of rural life.

Embracing Rural Tranquility

Nestled amid the rolling hills and verdant landscapes of the Mediterranean countryside, the experience of staying at a rustic farmstay offers a profound retreat from the frenetic pace of modern life. Here, the passage of time takes on a different cadence, guided not by the mechanical ticking of a clock but by the natural rhythms of the sun's journey across the sky. This setting allows visitors to disconnect from the chaos and immerse themselves in the gentle ambiance that pervades every corner of these farmstays, creating an idyllic backdrop for a serene and rejuvenating escape.

The Authentic Farm Experience

Perhaps the most captivating aspect of a rustic farmstay is the opportunity it affords to intimately engage with the authentic workings of a traditional Mediterranean farm. Guests have the privilege of witnessing and, if they choose, actively participating in the daily activities that sustain these agricultural communities. From tilling the fertile soil of the fields and nurturing the blossoms of orchards to the intimate chore of milking cows or goats, every act provides a window into the ancestral practices that have supported these communities for generations. Many farmstays extend a warm invitation for visitors to immerse themselves fully in this lifestyle, providing an invaluable chance to become an active part of the daily routines rather than just an observer.

Farm-to-Table Dining Delights

One of the crowning jewels of a rustic farmstay is the experience of indulging in farm-to-table dining. Imagine savoring dishes crafted from the freshest produce, plucked straight from the farm's own fields and gardens. Sun-ripened tomatoes bursting with flavor, fragrant herbs harvested just moments before, and artisanal cheeses infused with the essence of the surrounding landscape – these are the culinary treasures that grace your plate as you dine al fresco. Such meals transcend mere sustenance; they become a celebration of the land's bounty and the hands that lovingly tend to it. Dining in this environment is a sensory journey that encapsulates the essence of the Mediterranean's gastronomic culture.

Connecting with the Locals

Staying at a rustic farmstay opens a door to genuine interactions with the local community. The families who operate these farms are often eager to share their personal stories, ancestral traditions, and deep insights into the rich tapestry of the region's culture. Engaging in conversations while sipping on locally produced wine or leisurely strolling through fields creates moments of connection that are both heartwarming and enlightening. These shared experiences foster a sense of kinship that can extend well beyond your visit, leaving you with meaningful memories and friendships that endure.

Reconnecting with Nature

The Mediterranean countryside beckons to nature enthusiasts, and a rustic farmstay serves as an ideal base for exploration. Awaken to the melodious symphony of birdsong, embark on invigorating hikes along trails that unveil breathtaking vistas, or simply bask in the tranquility of fragrant gardens. After the sun sets, the absence of city lights unveils a panorama of stars, inviting you to reconnect with the cosmos in a profound and intimate way.

Creating Lasting Memories

More than a mere accommodation, a rustic farmstay is a canvas upon which you paint cherished memories. Be it the laughter shared while mastering traditional recipes, the satisfaction of nurturing plants from seed to harvest, or the quiet contemplation of a sunset over the fields, every moment becomes a brushstroke in the masterpiece of your Mediterranean journey. These experiences etch themselves into your heart, inviting you to carry them with you as you continue on your voyage.

Choosing the Right Farmstay

As you embark on this unique accommodation experience, selecting the right farmstay becomes paramount. Research options in the region you're visiting, read reviews, and consider the array of activities and amenities each farmstay offers. Some might provide opportunities for horseback riding, guided tours through local landmarks, or engaging workshops that delve into traditional crafts. Each farmstay has its own personality, and finding the one that resonates with your preferences and desires will enhance the overall depth of your Mediterranean encounter.

Here are some some examples of rustic farmstays along the Mediterranean countryside:

1. La Fattoria dell'Olio
Address: Via delle Colline, 123, Tuscany, Italy

Description: Nestled in the heart of Tuscany's picturesque countryside, La Fattoria dell'Olio offers a quintessential rustic farmstay experience. Surrounded by olive groves and vineyards, this charming agriturismo allows guests to unwind in traditional Tuscan style cottages. Participate in hands-on activities such as olive oil pressing and wine tasting, and savor authentic Italian cuisine prepared with locally sourced ingredients. The panoramic views of rolling hills and the scent of blooming wildflowers create a tranquil retreat.

2. Finca Verde
Address: Camí de Son Duri, 255, Mallorca, Spain

Description: Situated on the sun-drenched island of Mallorca, Finca Verde is a hidden gem for those seeking a rustic escape. This working farmstay immerses guests in the

Mediterranean lifestyle with cozy stone cottages surrounded by citrus and almond orchards. Engage in farm activities, from picking fresh oranges for breakfast to learning traditional pottery. Unwind by the pool or explore nearby hiking trails, all while enjoying the warm hospitality that Mallorca is known for.

3. Agriturismo Agrivilla I Pini
Address: Strada della Tognazza, 13, Tuscany, Italy

Description: Tucked away in the enchanting Chianti region of Tuscany, Agrivilla I Pini offers an authentic taste of rural Italy. The farmstay boasts well-appointed rooms in a historic villa, offering views of vineyards and cypress-lined landscapes. Indulge in farm-fresh meals accompanied by local wines, and immerse yourself in activities like grape harvesting and pasta-making workshops. The serene atmosphere and proximity to medieval villages make it an ideal base for exploring the region.

4. Quinta da Esperança
Address: Estrada Nacional 125, São Bartolomeu, Algarve, Portugal

Description: Quinta da Esperança in Portugal's Algarve region offers a rustic retreat with a touch of coastal charm. Set among lush gardens and fruit orchards, the farmstay features traditional cottages with whitewashed walls and terracotta roofs. Engage in farm activities like picking fresh figs and almonds, or unwind in the hammocks beneath olive trees. The nearby pristine beaches and traditional fishing villages offer a well-rounded Mediterranean experience.

5. Masseria Torre Coccaro
Address: Contrada Coccaro sn, Puglia, Italy

Description: Masseria Torre Coccaro, a luxurious yet authentic retreat in Puglia, Italy, combines rustic charm with modern comforts. Set amidst ancient olive trees and lush gardens, this farmstay boasts elegantly restored rooms and suites. Discover the farm's own olive oil production, relax by the pool, or take a cooking class using local ingredients. The property's proximity to the Adriatic Sea and historic towns adds cultural and coastal allure.

6. Mas de la Fouque
Address: Route du Petit Rhône, Camargue, France

Description: Mas de la Fouque, located in the unique Camargue region of southern France, offers a distinctive rustic farmstay experience. The elegant Provençal farmhouse is surrounded by marshlands, offering birdwatching and horseback riding opportunities. The farm's wetlands contribute to its own rice cultivation, and the on-site spa provides relaxation after exploring the natural beauty and the vibrant pink flamingos of Camargue.

7. Cappadocia Cave Land Hotel
Address: Aydınlı, Göreme, Nevşehir, Turkey

Description: Cappadocia Cave Land Hotel provides a rustic farmstay experience in the captivating landscapes of Cappadocia, Turkey. Set in a historic cave dwelling, the hotel blends ancient charm with modern amenities. Enjoy panoramic views of fairy chimneys and valleys, take part in pottery workshops, and relish traditional Turkish cuisine. The region's hot air balloon rides and ancient cave churches add an extra layer of adventure to your stay.

Staying at a rustic farmstay in the Mediterranean countryside is an invitation to step away from the ordinary and embrace the extraordinary. It's a chance to disconnect from the digital noise and reconnect with the rhythms of nature, agriculture, and community. By choosing this distinctive form of accommodation, you're not just finding a place to sleep; you're opening yourself up to a transformative experience that will forever remain etched in your travel memories. So, pack your bags, leave the urban frenzy behind, and embark on a journey that will bring you closer to the heart of the Mediterranean spirit.

Homestays and Cultural Exchanges

Living with Locals on the Island of Crete

One of the most enriching ways to experience the Mediterranean's authentic charm is by immersing yourself in local life through homestays and cultural exchanges. While there are numerous destinations that offer this opportunity, the island of Crete stands out as a particularly exceptional location for such an experience. Nestled in the southern part of the Aegean Sea, Crete is not only renowned for its stunning landscapes and historical significance but also for its warm and welcoming inhabitants who are eager to share their traditions, stories, and way of life with visitors.

Connecting with the Heart of Cretan Hospitality

The Cretans are renowned for their renowned hospitality, known as "philoxenia" in Greek, which translates to a love for strangers. This sentiment has been passed down through generations and is deeply ingrained in the island's culture. When you choose a homestay on Crete, you're not just booking a room; you're entering the heart of a Cretan family's home and becoming part of their daily rhythm.

The Homestay Experience

Homestays on Crete offer a unique opportunity to connect with locals on a personal level. Many families open their doors to travelers, providing them with a comfortable room and a genuine insight into Cretan life. Picture waking up to the aroma of freshly baked bread and enjoying breakfast made with ingredients harvested from the family garden. This experience allows you to appreciate the simplicity of life while connecting with your hosts through shared meals, stories, and activities.

Learning the Art of Cretan Cuisine

One of the highlights of a homestay on Crete is undoubtedly the chance to learn about and savor the island's traditional cuisine. Cretan cuisine is known for its emphasis on fresh, locally sourced ingredients, and many families take pride in passing down recipes that have been cherished for generations. Guests often have the opportunity to participate in cooking classes, where they learn to create dishes like "dakos" (a traditional Cretan salad), "sfakianopita" (cheese-filled pastry), and "kleftiko" (slow-cooked lamb).

Participating in Local Traditions

Staying with a Cretan family opens the door to experiencing local traditions and festivities firsthand. Depending on the time of year, you might find yourself taking part in grape harvests, olive oil production, or traditional music and dance events. These moments allow you to not only witness but actively engage in the vibrant tapestry of Cretan culture.

Exploring the Island's Hidden Gems

Your hosts, who know the island intimately, can guide you to off-the-beaten-path destinations that you might otherwise miss. Whether it's a secluded beach with crystal-clear waters, a charming mountain village, or a hidden chapel nestled amidst the olive groves, their insights will lead you to some of Crete's most cherished and less touristy spots.

Cultural Exchange and Lasting Memories

A homestay on Crete is more than just a place to rest your head; it's an opportunity for genuine cultural exchange. By sharing in the daily routines, stories, and traditions of your hosts, you'll leave with a deeper understanding of Cretan life and an enriched perspective on the Mediterranean way of living. The friendships formed during these experiences often extend beyond your stay, leaving you with lasting memories and connections to cherish for years to come.

In conclusion, a homestay on the island of Crete offers an unparalleled opportunity to engage with the local culture, cuisine, and way of life. By choosing this immersive experience, you'll not only explore the beauty of the island's landscapes but also create lasting connections with its people. The memories you make while living with locals will undoubtedly become the heart of your Mediterranean travel adventure.

Joining Cooking Classes in Provence

One of the most authentic and immersive ways to experience the Mediterranean is by participating in homestays and cultural exchanges. These opportunities allow travelers to connect deeply with the local way of life, gaining insights into traditions, customs, and daily routines that might otherwise remain hidden from the casual tourist's eye. Among the many options available, joining cooking classes in the charming region of Provence stands out as a delightful and mouthwatering experience.

Culinary Exploration in the Heart of Provence

Provence, nestled in the southeastern part of France, is renowned for its stunning landscapes, aromatic lavender fields, and picturesque villages. However, beyond its visual allure, Provence boasts a culinary heritage that is equally captivating. The region's cuisine is characterized by fresh, locally sourced ingredients, fragrant herbs, and a distinct Mediterranean influence. From olive oil to sun-ripened tomatoes and fragrant rosemary, Provencal cuisine is a celebration of flavors that reflect the land's bountiful offerings.

A Hands-On Adventure

For travelers seeking a hands-on adventure, enrolling in cooking classes within a local homestay is an exceptional way to immerse themselves in the gastronomic culture of Provence. These classes are often hosted by passionate home cooks who open their kitchens and hearts to share their culinary secrets. As you step into the warm and inviting atmosphere of a Provencal home, you'll find yourself surrounded by the aromas of fresh herbs and the anticipation of crafting traditional dishes.

Exploring the Market: A Lesson in Ingredients

Before diving into the cooking process, many classes start with a visit to a local market. Here, you'll accompany your host to select the finest and freshest ingredients for your culinary creations. The market is not only a place to source ingredients but also a treasure trove of sensory experiences.

The vibrant colors of fruits and vegetables, the rich scent of freshly baked bread, and the cheerful banter of locals all contribute to the immersive encounter.

From Garden to Table: Cooking Provencal Delights

Back in the kitchen, you'll have the chance to roll up your sleeves and become a part of the culinary magic. Under the guidance of your expert host, you'll learn to prepare iconic Provencal dishes that have been passed down through generations. Ratatouille, bouillabaisse, and pissaladière are just a few examples of the delectable creations you might master during your cooking class.

What makes these experiences truly special is the emphasis on traditional methods and techniques. From chopping vegetables to simmering stews, you'll gain a firsthand understanding of the nuances that contribute to Provencal flavors. As you work side by side with your host, you'll also have the opportunity to engage in meaningful conversations, exchanging stories and cultural insights.

A Feast for the Senses

As your culinary creations come together, the kitchen transforms into a space of celebration. The table is set, and the dishes you've lovingly prepared take center stage. The meal becomes not just a feast for the palate, but also a feast for the senses and a testament to the shared moments of cooking and camaraderie.

Breaking bread with your host and fellow travelers is an intimate experience that goes beyond the act of eating. It's a moment of connection, where different cultures and backgrounds converge over a shared appreciation for good food and genuine hospitality. The bonds forged during these cooking classes often endure long after the meal has been savored.

Bringing Provence Home

Participating in cooking classes during a homestay in Provence offers more than just a culinary lesson. It's an opportunity to capture the essence of a region and its people through the art of food. As you return home, you'll carry with you not only recipes and cooking techniques but also a deeper understanding of Provencal culture and a lasting connection to the friends you've made along the way.

In the end, the journey of joining cooking classes in Provence transcends the act of cooking itself. It becomes a memory etched in flavors, aromas, and laughter – a memory that continues to inspire your culinary adventures long after you've bid adieu to the sun-soaked shores of the Mediterranean.

Living with Locals in the Amalfi Coast: Embracing Authentic Italian Hospitality

The Amalfi Coast, often referred to as the "Divine Coast," is a region that embodies the epitome of Mediterranean beauty. Its rugged cliffs, turquoise waters, and charming villages create a postcard-perfect landscape that has captured the hearts of travelers for generations. But beyond its natural allure, the Amalfi Coast offers a unique opportunity to go beyond the surface and truly immerse oneself in the local way of life through homestays and cultural exchanges.

Embracing the Rhythms of Amalfi Coast Life

Imagine waking up to the gentle symphony of waves crashing against the rocks and the invigorating scent of lemon trees wafting through your window. This is the reality of staying with a local family on the Amalfi Coast. Homestays here are more than just accommodations; they are gateways to experiencing the region's culture, traditions, and warm-hearted hospitality.

The Amalfi Coast is dotted with quaint villages that maintain a strong connection to their heritage. Staying in one of these villages offers a glimpse into the daily lives of its residents. You might find yourself engaged in activities that have been passed down through generations, such as fishing with local fishermen or helping tend to the fragrant vineyards that dot the landscape.

Culinary Explorations and Traditional Celebrations

One of the highlights of living with locals on the Amalfi Coast is the opportunity to savor authentic Italian cuisine. Imagine sitting down to a home-cooked meal prepared using age-old family recipes, where each dish is a celebration of local flavors and traditions. From hand-rolled pasta to succulent seafood caught just offshore, every bite tells a story of the region's bounty.

But the experience doesn't end with just the meals. Engaging with your hosts might involve learning the art of crafting pasta from scratch or assisting in preparing traditional desserts. As you chop, stir, and sizzle alongside them, you'll gain insights into the culinary secrets that have been cherished for generations.

Participating in local celebrations is another way to forge connections with the Amalfi Coast's vibrant culture. You might find yourself dancing in the streets during a festival, joining in on a traditional tarantella dance, or even trying your hand at making limoncello, the zesty lemon liqueur that's a regional specialty.

Creating Lasting Bonds

Living with locals on the Amalfi Coast not only offers a deeper understanding of the region's culture but also creates lasting connections. As you share stories, laughter, and meals, you become more than just a tourist passing through. You become a member of the community, welcomed into the heart of Amalfi Coast life.

As you bid farewell to your hosts, you'll carry with you not just memories of breathtaking landscapes but also the warmth and hospitality of the people who call this stunning coastline home. The experience of living with locals on the Amalfi Coast transcends mere sightseeing; it's an immersion into a way of life that's as rich and vibrant as the land itself.

The Amalfi Coast is a destination that captures the imagination with its natural beauty, but it's the opportunity to live like a local that truly sets it apart. Homestays on this divine stretch of coastline allow you to dive into the rhythm of Amalfi Coast life, from fishing with locals to savoring homemade Italian delicacies. By embracing this unique way of travel, you don't just see the Amalfi Coast – you become a part of its story, forging connections that will remain with you long after you've returned home.

Village Hospitality in the Greek Islands: Embracing Authentic Island Life

The Greek Islands have long held a special allure for travelers seeking a blend of stunning landscapes, ancient history, and vibrant cultures. However, beyond the postcard-perfect beaches and historic sites, these islands are also home to tight-knit communities that have preserved their traditions for generations. For those seeking a more immersive and intimate experience, village hospitality on the Greek Islands offers a chance to become a part of these communities and truly embrace the local way of life.

Becoming a Part of Island Communities

Imagine waking up in a traditional whitewashed village on the iconic island of Santorini, where cobblestone streets wind their way through clusters of charming houses. Instead of being a tourist passing through, you become an honorary member of the community, welcomed into the daily rhythms of island life.

Engaging with the locals might involve participating in activities that are deeply rooted in tradition. Joining the fishermen as they set out to sea at dawn, you'll gain insights into a trade that has sustained generations. Tending to olive groves, an essential part of Greek agricultural heritage, provides not only a hands-on experience but also an understanding of the land's significance to the locals.

Cooking Up Traditions and Sharing Stories

Greek culture is intricately woven with a rich culinary tapestry. Participating in cooking activities during your village stay unveils the secrets of authentic Greek cuisine. Picture yourself gathering fresh ingredients from local markets, learning how to shape traditional dishes like moussaka and spanakopita, and relishing the joy of sharing a meal that you've helped prepare.

But village hospitality is more than just activities – it's about forging connections through shared experiences. Sitting down to a meal of grilled fish, freshly picked olives, and hearty Greek salad, you'll find yourself engaged in conversations that transcend language barriers. These moments offer a glimpse into the islanders' lives, their histories, and the stories that have been passed down through generations.

Festivals, Music, and Dance

Participating in local celebrations is a highlight of village hospitality on the Greek Islands. Imagine joining in on a traditional Greek dance circle during a village festival. The lively music, swirling dances, and spirited atmosphere create bonds that extend far beyond your time on the island. These moments of unity and joy connect you with the essence of Greek culture and its celebration of life.

Creating Lifelong Memories

Village hospitality on the Greek Islands is not just a temporary stay; it's an opportunity to create memories that will stay with you forever. By immersing yourself in the rhythms of local life, you'll gain insights that go beyond guidebook descriptions. You'll develop an appreciation for the islanders' deep connection to their land, their traditions, and their communities.

As you bid farewell to your hosts, you'll realize that your time spent living like a local has woven you into the fabric of island life. The connections you've formed, the stories you've shared, and the experiences you've had will forever be a part of your Greek Island journey.

Village hospitality on the Greek Islands offers a window into a world where tradition, community, and natural beauty come together in harmony. It's a chance to step beyond the typical tourist experience and immerse yourself in the lives of those who call these islands home. From cooking traditional dishes to dancing at local festivals, the memories you create will be more than travel snapshots – they'll be snapshots of moments lived as a part of something bigger, something deeply rooted in the history and culture of the Greek Islands.

Rural Retreats in the Moroccan Countryside: Discovering the Mediterranean Blend

While discussions of Mediterranean travel often conjure images of iconic European coastlines, the northern coast of Morocco offers a unique blend of cultures, landscapes, and experiences. Far from the bustling cities, this region presents travelers with the opportunity to step back in time and experience the Mediterranean in a whole new light. Rural retreats in the Moroccan countryside provide a gateway to the slower pace of life and the vibrant blend of Mediterranean and Moroccan influences.

Exploring the Moroccan Countryside

Imagine finding yourself in a quaint coastal village in Morocco, surrounded by the striking contrast of azure waters and rugged landscapes. Here, you have the chance to stay in a traditional riad, a Moroccan-style house with an interior courtyard that exudes tranquility and authenticity. This setting becomes the backdrop for your journey into the heart of Moroccan life.

Daily routines take on new significance as you engage in age-old practices. Participating in baking sessions to create fresh bread in communal ovens is a testament to the communal spirit that binds the community together. Learning the intricate art of crafting colorful mosaics, an ancient tradition passed down through generations, provides a window into the region's artistic heritage.

A Blend of Mediterranean and Moroccan Cultures

The northern coastline of Morocco is a melting pot of cultures, where Mediterranean influences blend seamlessly with Moroccan traditions. Engaging with the local Berber communities sheds light on the intricate tapestry that has been woven over centuries of trade, exploration, and cultural exchange.

Imagine conversing with locals who speak not only of Moroccan traditions but also of the Mediterranean connections that have shaped their identity. Discovering the shared elements between Mediterranean and Moroccan cuisines – the use of fresh ingredients, aromatic spices, and vibrant colors – provides a taste of the rich cultural intersection that defines this region.

Connecting with the Past and Present

Staying in the Moroccan countryside is an opportunity to experience life at a different pace, one that values the art of slow living and meaningful connections. The absence of modern distractions allows for a deeper engagement with your surroundings and the people you encounter.

As you explore the rugged landscapes and engage in time-honored traditions, you'll develop a profound appreciation for the interplay between the Mediterranean and Moroccan influences. This appreciation extends to the everyday interactions with the locals, whose stories reflect the cultural dialogue that continues to shape this region.

Preserving Traditions for the Future

The experience of rural retreats in the Moroccan countryside is not just a journey into the past; it's an investment in the future. By embracing the traditions and way of life of the local communities, you contribute to the preservation of cultural heritage. Your presence becomes a testament to the importance of celebrating diversity and the bonds that connect people across geographical and cultural boundaries.

Exploring the northern coastline of Morocco is an exploration of the Mediterranean that often goes unnoticed. Rural retreats in this region offer a glimpse into a world where traditions, landscapes, and cultures converge to create a unique tapestry. By immersing yourself in the rhythms of rural life, you gain insights into the interconnectedness of Mediterranean and Moroccan influences. The memories you make and the connections you forge will remind you that the Mediterranean experience is not limited to European coastlines; it encompasses a rich and diverse cultural mosaic that spans continents and history.

Harbor Life in the Turkish Riviera: Unveiling Coastal Traditions

The Turkish Riviera, also known as the Turquoise Coast, is renowned for its stunning beaches, ancient ruins, and vibrant markets. While these attractions draw visitors from around the world, there's an opportunity to go beyond the tourist hotspots and delve into the heart of coastal life. Embracing harbor life on the Turkish Riviera allows you to immerse yourself in the traditions and rhythms of the Mediterranean.

Living with Fishing Families

Imagine staying in a picturesque village like Kas or Bodrum, nestled along the Turkish coastline. Instead of merely observing the sea, you become a part of it by joining a local fishing family on their traditional boats. Rising with the sun, you embark on a journey that has sustained coastal communities for generations – the art of fishing.

As you cast your nets and witness the daily catch, you gain a newfound appreciation for the connection between these communities and the bountiful Mediterranean waters. This hands-on experience offers insights into the life of a fisherman, the challenges they face, and the traditions they uphold.

Sharing Coastal Culinary Traditions

Engaging with local families on the Turkish Riviera means more than just fishing – it also means sharing meals that reflect the region's coastal heritage. Picture sitting around a communal table laden with freshly caught seafood, aromatic spices, and an array of mezze. Each dish tells a story of the sea, the land, and the vibrant culture that thrives along the coast.

As you savor the flavors of traditional Turkish cuisine, you'll discover the intricate balance between the simplicity of ingredients and the complexity of tastes. Sharing these meals with your hosts provides a deeper understanding of the culinary traditions that have evolved over centuries.

Celebrating Maritime Culture

The Turkish Riviera's history is intertwined with the sea, and this maritime heritage is celebrated through local festivals and customs. Imagine joining in on a local celebration where you're surrounded by lively music, colorful costumes, and the rhythmic footwork of traditional dances.

These festivals not only provide an opportunity for celebration but also offer insights into the significance of the sea in the lives of the locals. Engaging with these customs allows you to connect with the heart of coastal traditions and understand the integral role that the Mediterranean has played in shaping the cultural identity of the region.

Creating Bonds and Memories

By living with fishing families and participating in coastal traditions, you'll create bonds that transcend language barriers and cultural differences. The shared experiences, whether out on the water, around the table, or during festive celebrations, foster a sense of camaraderie and unity. These connections become the foundation of lifelong memories that will forever be associated with the Turkish Riviera.

Harbor life on the Turkish Riviera offers a unique perspective on Mediterranean travel. It's a journey into the heart of coastal communities, where traditions, culinary delights, and maritime heritage come together to create a vibrant tapestry. By immersing yourself in the rhythms of life along the coast, you'll gain insights into the interplay between human culture and the natural beauty of the Mediterranean. The memories you make and the connections you forge will serve as a reminder that the

Mediterranean experience is not only about sightseeing, but also about becoming a part of the living heritage of the region.

Exploring Agritourism in Sicily: A Journey Through Mediterranean Flavors

Sicily, the largest island in the Mediterranean, is a land of diverse landscapes, rich history, and a culinary heritage that's second to none. Beyond the bustling cities, the heart of the island invites travelers to experience agritourism – a captivating blend of agriculture and tourism that offers a unique perspective on the Mediterranean way of life.

The Charm of Sicilian Farmhouses

Imagine arriving at a traditional Sicilian farmhouse surrounded by vineyards, olive groves, and fragrant citrus orchards. This picturesque setting becomes your home as you delve into the heart of agritourism. The farmhouses, often centuries-old, exude rustic charm and offer a genuine escape from the modern world.

Staying on a Sicilian farmhouse is a journey into the heart of Sicilian rural life. Each sunrise brings the promise of new adventures – whether it's participating in olive harvesting, learning the art of cheese-making from local artisans, or strolling through the vineyards as the grapes ripen.

Harvesting Sicilian Bounty

Sicily's agritourism experience goes beyond passive observation; it's about active participation in the island's agricultural traditions. Imagine joining farmers in the olive groves, where you'll learn the ancient techniques of harvesting and pressing olives to produce the golden elixir of Sicilian olive oil.

The grape harvest season offers another opportunity to engage with the land. Grape stomping, an age-old practice that blends fun and tradition, lets you experience the winemaking process firsthand. You'll gain a deep appreciation for the skill and dedication required to produce Sicily's renowned wines.

Savoring the Sicilian Table

At the heart of agritourism is the celebration of food – a cornerstone of Mediterranean culture. Imagine sitting down to a meal prepared from ingredients sourced directly from the land around you. From freshly harvested olives and sun-ripened tomatoes to artisanal cheeses and cured meats, every bite is a symphony of flavors that tell the story of the Sicilian countryside.

Participating in cooking workshops with local chefs introduces you to the art of crafting Sicilian dishes. The scent of garlic and herbs fills the air as you learn to make pasta from scratch, prepare arancini, or bake the iconic cannoli. These experiences offer more than just recipes; they provide a profound connection to the island's culinary heritage.

Connecting with Sicilian Traditions

Agritourism in Sicily offers more than just a vacation – it's an opportunity to connect with the traditions that have shaped the island's identity. Engaging with local farmers, artisans, and chefs provides insights into their daily lives, their histories, and the passion they bring to their crafts.

Exploring the charming towns nearby allows you to experience the local culture beyond the farm's borders. Imagine strolling through vibrant markets, where stalls overflow with colorful produce, handcrafted goods, and traditional delicacies. Engaging with local communities during festivals, parades, and celebrations offers a window into the spirit of Sicily.

A Lasting Connection

As your time in Sicily's agritourism comes to an end, you'll realize that you've created more than just memories – you've formed a lasting connection to the land, its people, and its traditions. The experience of agritourism encapsulates the essence of the Mediterranean way of life – the deep bond between people, the land, and the nourishing bounty it provides.

Exploring agritourism in Sicily offers a multi-sensory journey through the heart of the Mediterranean. From the rustic charm of traditional farmhouses to the hands-on experiences of olive harvesting and wine-making, each moment is an opportunity to connect with the land and its traditions. Sharing meals with local farmers and chefs provides a taste of the island's culinary heritage, while engaging with local communities and celebrations offers insights into Sicily's vibrant culture. Ultimately, agritourism is a pathway to a deeper understanding of the Mediterranean's rich heritage and the connections that bind people to the land they call home.

Conclusion: Embracing the Mediterranean Tapestry

The Mediterranean is more than just a geographical region; it's a tapestry woven from diverse cultures, landscapes, and traditions. From the Amalfi Coast to the Greek Islands, the Moroccan countryside to the Turkish Riviera, and Sicilian agritourism, the experiences of living with locals offer a profound understanding of what makes the Mediterranean so captivating.

Each of these unique encounters goes beyond the ordinary tourist experience. They provide a chance to step into the daily lives of the people who call these places home, to share in their traditions, and to forge connections that transcend boundaries. Through homestays, cultural exchanges, and active participation, travelers become more than mere observers – they become participants in the rich heritage of the Mediterranean.

The Mediterranean is a meeting point of civilizations, where diverse influences have intermingled to create a cultural mosaic that is as dynamic as it is beautiful. By immersing oneself in village life, embracing coastal traditions, and engaging with local customs, travelers gain a deeper appreciation for the interplay of history, culture, and the natural world.

As you bid farewell to the Amalfi Coast, the Greek Islands, the Moroccan countryside, the Turkish Riviera, and the rustic farms of Sicily, you carry with you not only memories but also a newfound understanding of the profound connections that tie the Mediterranean together. These experiences serve as a reminder that the true essence of travel lies not just in seeing new places, but in forming bonds that transcend time and place.

Ultimately, the magic of the Mediterranean lies not only in its landscapes of sun-soaked shores and historic ruins but also in the warmth of its people, the authenticity of its traditions, and the richness of its cultures. By living with locals and embracing their way of life, you become a part of this tapestry, leaving an indelible mark on your own journey through the Mediterranean.

Chapter 6: Capturing Memories - Photography and Souvenirs

Photography Tips for Stunning Mediterranean Landscapes

Photography has the power to freeze a moment in time and transport us back to the beauty of a place. The Mediterranean region, with its breathtaking landscapes, vibrant colors, and rich cultural heritage, offers an abundance of photographic opportunities. Whether you're a seasoned photographer or just starting out, capturing the essence of the Mediterranean can be a rewarding endeavor. Here are some photography tips to help you make the most of your visual journey:

Capturing Sunrise on the Amalfi Coast

The Amalfi Coast, a UNESCO World Heritage site in Italy, is renowned for its dramatic cliffs, charming villages, and stunning seascapes. One of the most magical moments to capture here is the sunrise. The golden light illuminates the pastel-colored buildings and dances on the azure waters, creating a surreal and enchanting atmosphere.

- Plan Ahead: Research the best vantage points for capturing the sunrise. Popular spots include the towns of Positano, Ravello, and Amalfi itself. Arrive early to secure your spot and set up your equipment.

- Use a Tripod: Shooting in low light conditions requires stability. A sturdy tripod will help you achieve sharp, clear images without the risk of camera shake.

- Golden Hour Magic: The hour just before sunrise offers a soft, warm light that can transform your photographs. Experiment with different compositions to include iconic elements like the winding roads, bougainvillaea-covered walls, and the sea stretching out to the horizon.

- Manual Mode Mastery: Take control of your camera settings. Use a low ISO to minimize noise and a wide aperture (low f-number) to create a shallow depth of field, making your subject stand out against the dreamy background.

- Long Exposures: If you encounter water, consider using a slow shutter speed to capture the movement of waves or create a silky effect in the water.

Framing the Sunset at Santorini's Oia

Santorini, Greece, is synonymous with romance and beauty. The village of Oia, perched on the caldera's edge, provides an exquisite setting for capturing the sun's descent into the Aegean Sea. The iconic blue-domed churches, whitewashed buildings, and the sparkling sea serve as the perfect backdrop for your sunset shots.

- Arrive Early: Just like with sunrise photography, arriving early ensures you secure a prime location for your shoot. The popularity of Oia's sunsets can lead to crowded spaces.

- Experiment with Composition: While capturing the classic sunset-over-the-sea shot is a must, don't hesitate to explore different angles and viewpoints. Incorporate architectural elements or silhouettes of people to add a sense of scale and context.

- Filters for Drama: Graduated neutral density filters can help balance the exposure between the bright sky and the darker foreground, preventing overexposed skies or underexposed landscapes.

- Bracketing for Range: To capture a wider range of light in scenes with high contrast, consider bracketing your shots. This involves taking multiple shots at different exposures and later merging them for a perfectly exposed image.

- Stay After Sunset: Don't pack up as soon as the sun dips below the horizon. The afterglow can paint the sky with hues of pink, purple, and gold, creating a spectacular canvas for your photographs.

Exploring the Lush Vineyards of Tuscany

Tuscany, Italy, is renowned not only for its artistic heritage but also for its rolling hills adorned with vineyards and charming farmhouses. Capturing the essence of this rustic beauty requires a different approach.

- Embrace the Magic Hour: The soft, warm light during the golden hour just after sunrise and before sunset can add a touch of enchantment to your vineyard shots. The gentle sunlight enhances the textures of the grapevines and the landscape.

- Capture the Details: Don't shy away from close-ups. Capture the intricate patterns of the grape leaves, the textures of the soil, and the weathered wood of the wine barrels.

- Incorporate Leading Lines: The rows of grapevines create natural leading lines that draw the viewer's eye into the scene. Experiment with different angles to make the most of this natural composition element.

- Human Element: Including people, whether they are vineyard workers or visitors, can add a sense of scale and narrative to your photographs. Candid shots of winemaking processes or a shared meal can evoke a sense of the region's lifestyle.

Sailing into the Aegean: Capturing Seascapes and Islands

The Mediterranean's crystal-clear waters and picturesque islands provide ample opportunities for capturing stunning seascapes and coastal scenes.

- Play with Reflections: When shooting on or near the water, take advantage of the reflective surfaces. Capture the vibrant colors of boats and buildings mirrored in the calm sea.

- Use a Polarizing Filter: A polarizing filter can reduce glare from the water's surface and enhance the colors of the sky and sea. It can also add depth and contrast to your images.

- Experiment with Panoramas: The sweeping coastal views and islands dotted across the horizon are perfect candidates for panoramic shots. Use the panorama mode on your camera or stitch multiple images together during post-processing.

- Highlighting Architecture: When capturing coastal villages, focus on the unique architecture. Whitewashed buildings against the blue backdrop can create a captivating contrast.

- Seize the Twilight: The transition between day and night, known as the "blue hour," can add a serene and ethereal quality to your seascapes. The soft blue hues complement the Mediterranean's ambiance.

Cinematic Views in Dubrovnik's City Walls

Dubrovnik, Croatia, is a city of historic charm, encircled by ancient walls that offer breathtaking panoramic views of the Adriatic Sea and red-roofed buildings.

- Capture Layers: Utilize the city's layered landscape by framing shots that show the terracotta rooftops below, the shimmering sea beyond, and the distant islands on the horizon.

- Golden Hour Magic: During sunrise and sunset, the sunlight casts a warm and soft glow on the city. Experiment with different angles to capture the play of light and shadow on the cobblestone streets and walls.

- Explore Narrow Streets: Wander beyond the main squares to find charming alleys and staircases. These secluded spots offer opportunities for intimate and intriguing compositions.

- Silhouette Skylines: As the sun sets behind the city walls, capture striking silhouettes of people against the orange and pink hues of the sky. The city's distinctive architecture can create dramatic profiles.

Mesmerizing Mosaic of Malta's Blue Grotto

The Blue Grotto in Malta is a natural wonder known for its vibrant blue waters and intricate cave formations. Capturing its beauty requires an understanding of light and the underwater environment.

- Snorkeling Photography: If you're comfortable with underwater photography, snorkel in the Blue Grotto's clear waters to capture the play of sunlight on the water's surface and the mesmerizing blue hues underneath.

- Above the Surface: While capturing underwater shots can be challenging, focusing on the grotto's entrance and the boats approaching it can also create captivating compositions.

- Timing is Key: Visit the Blue Grotto during mid-morning when the sun's rays penetrate the caves and illuminate the water. The interplay of light and shadow adds depth to your images.

- Use Waterproof Housing: If you're equipped with a waterproof camera or housing, experiment with half-in, half-out shots that showcase both the stunning underwater world and the grotto's rocky surroundings.

- Post-Processing Enhancement: Adjusting the color balance and saturation during post-processing can help bring out the true shades of blue and enhance the enchantment of the grotto.

Exploring the Hidden Coves of the French Riviera

The French Riviera, or Côte d'Azur, is celebrated for its glamorous beaches and azure waters. However, hidden along its rugged coastline are enchanting coves and secluded beaches that offer a different perspective of the Mediterranean.

- Seek Out Secluded Spots: Research and ask locals to discover lesser-known coves that might not be crowded with tourists. These hidden gems provide an intimate and tranquil setting for your photography.

- Play with Sunlight and Shadows: The dappled sunlight filtering through the foliage onto the beach can create a captivating interplay of light and shadow. Experiment with different angles to capture this effect.

Cinematic Views in Dubrovnik, Croatia

Dubrovnik, often referred to as the "Pearl of the Adriatic," is a treasure trove of historic architecture, ancient city walls, and stunning coastal vistas. As the sun sets, the city's terracotta roofs and limestone streets are bathed in a warm, golden glow.

- Utilize Leading Lines: The winding streets and staircases of Dubrovnik's old town provide excellent opportunities to use leading lines to guide the viewer's eye through your photograph.
- Capture the City Walls: The city's renowned walls offer panoramic views of both the Adriatic Sea and the charming cityscape. Consider using a wide-angle lens to encompass these sweeping vistas.

Majestic Cliffs of the Costa Brava, Spain

The Costa Brava in Spain boasts rugged cliffs that meet the sparkling Mediterranean sea. These dramatic landscapes offer a mix of turquoise waters, lush vegetation, and ancient ruins.

- Experiment with Drone Photography: If possible, use a drone to capture breathtaking aerial shots of the coastline. Drones provide a unique perspective that can highlight the scale and beauty of the cliffs.

- Embrace the Magic Hour: The hour just after sunrise and before sunset, known as the "golden hour," casts a warm and soft light that enhances the natural beauty of the cliffs and the sea.

Ancient Ruins and Azure Waters in Malta

Malta's unique blend of ancient history and coastal charm creates a fascinating backdrop for photography. The island's historic sites, such as the ancient city of Mdina and the

Megalithic Temples, offer a captivating contrast against the vibrant blue Mediterranean waters.

- Capture Cultural Contrasts: Frame your shots to juxtapose ancient architecture with the contemporary energy of the sea, showcasing the dynamic nature of the Mediterranean's heritage.

- Underwater Photography: Malta's clear waters are perfect for underwater photography. Capture the marine life, vibrant coral, and even shipwrecks for a different perspective of the Mediterranean's beauty.

Exploring Cinque Terre's Vernazza in the Golden Hour

The charming village of Vernazza in the Cinque Terre region of Italy is a picturesque gem that comes alive during the golden hour. The warm, soft light of this period bathes the colorful buildings and the tranquil harbor in a captivating glow. To make the most of your photography in Vernazza:

- Research the Schedule: Find out when the golden hour occurs, as the timing changes throughout the year. It's typically shortly after sunrise and before sunset.

- Discover Unique Angles: Experiment with different viewpoints to capture the village from unique perspectives. This might involve climbing to higher vantage points or getting closer to the water's edge.

- Incorporate Human Elements: The presence of people can add a sense of scale and life to your photos.

Capture locals going about their daily routines or visitors enjoying the scenery.

- Play with Shadows: During the golden hour, shadows become longer and more interesting. Incorporate these shadows creatively into your compositions.

Cultural Richness in Marrakech's Medina

Marrakech, Morocco, is a vibrant city known for its bustling markets, intricate architecture, and rich cultural heritage. Capturing the essence of the medina requires an eye for detail and a flair for capturing moments.

- Bustling Bazaars: Explore the medina's bustling souks, where vibrant colors, textiles, and handicrafts abound. Candid shots of vendors and shoppers haggling can showcase the lively atmosphere.

- Architectural Marvels: The medina is a treasure trove of stunning architecture, from the intricate patterns of the doorways to the grandeur of the palaces. Focus on the details that characterize Moroccan design.

- Street Portraits: Engage with locals and seek permission to capture their portraits. The diverse faces and traditional clothing can tell stories of the people who make Marrakech's medina come alive.

- Play with Light and Shadows: The narrow alleys and courtyards often create interesting interplays of light and shadow. Capture these dynamic contrasts to add depth to your photographs.

Azure Horizons of the Greek Islands

The Greek Islands, scattered throughout the Aegean and Ionian Seas, offer idyllic landscapes of white-washed buildings against the backdrop of the endless blue sea. Capturing this timeless beauty requires an appreciation for simplicity and harmony.

- Whitewashed Wonders: Frame shots that emphasize the iconic white buildings against the clear blue sky and sea. The contrast creates a clean and timeless composition.

- Island Hopping: Each Greek island has its unique character. Capture the distinct architecture, colors, and landscapes of islands like Mykonos, Santorini, and Crete.

- Local Life: Beyond the postcard scenes, focus on the daily lives of the locals. Photograph fishermen, artisans, and tavern owners as they go about their routines.

- Dusk and Dawn: Just before sunrise and after sunset, the soft light bathes the islands in a magical glow. The tranquil moments between day and night create a serene and contemplative atmosphere.

Remember, the Mediterranean's appeal lies not only in its picturesque landscapes but also in the stories it tells. As you capture moments and scenes, aim to convey the emotions, history, and culture that define each place. Your photography can become a window through which others can experience the Mediterranean's charm and allure.

Souvenir Shopping and Local Crafts

When you travel to the Mediterranean, you're not just immersing yourself in stunning landscapes and rich history; you're also stepping into a world of vibrant crafts and unique souvenirs that tell stories of the region's culture and heritage. From bustling Turkish bazaars to the artistic heart of Andalusia, the Mediterranean offers a treasure trove of artisanal delights waiting to be discovered.

Unearthing Artisanal Treasures in Turkish Bazaars

No trip to the Mediterranean is complete without experiencing the bustling energy and enchanting chaos of a Turkish bazaar. These vibrant markets, also known as "souks," are scattered throughout Turkey and offer an immersive glimpse into the country's age-old trading traditions.

As you step into a Turkish bazaar, prepare to be swept away by a sensory overload of colors, scents, and sounds. Rows upon rows of shops are filled with an array of goods, from intricate carpets and textiles to ornate lanterns and jewelry. One of the most captivating aspects of these bazaars is the opportunity to witness skilled artisans at work. Watch as silversmiths craft intricate jewelry, glassblowers mold delicate ornaments, and leatherworkers create beautifully embossed accessories.

Among the most sought-after souvenirs are the world-famous Turkish carpets and kilims. These exquisite handwoven pieces are a testament to the country's longstanding weaving tradition. Each carpet tells a story through its intricate patterns and vibrant hues, making them not just a beautiful addition to your home, but a tangible piece of Turkish history. Remember to engage with the merchants, haggling playfully and respectfully – it's all part of the experience. Take your time to explore the bazaar, allowing the atmosphere to guide you to unique treasures that resonate with your sense of style.

Collecting Ceramics and Pottery from Andalusia

The sun-soaked region of Andalusia, in southern Spain, is a haven for art and culture enthusiasts. Its charming towns and cities are not only adorned with stunning architecture but also known for their rich tradition of ceramics and pottery.

Strolling through the cobbled streets of cities like Seville, Granada, and Cordoba, you'll come across an array of pottery workshops and boutiques. The craftsmanship here is deeply rooted in Moorish influence, and the intricate designs often reflect the region's historical blend of cultures.

One of the most iconic types of Andalusian pottery is "azulejos," which are decorative ceramic tiles. These tiles are often found adorning the facades of buildings, telling stories through intricate patterns and vibrant colors. Many shops offer hand-painted azulejos, allowing you to bring a piece of Andalusia's artistic heritage back home. Consider using them to create a stunning mosaic or decorative piece.

Apart from tiles, Andalusia is renowned for its vibrant ceramics, ranging from delicately painted plates to intricately designed vases and bowls. Many of these pieces feature traditional motifs like the "azahar" (orange blossom), evoking the scents of the region's iconic orange groves.

When collecting ceramics and pottery from Andalusia, take the time to learn about the stories behind the designs. Many artisans are passionate about sharing the history and significance of their craft. Whether you're purchasing a small trinket or a larger centerpiece, these pieces will serve as lasting reminders of your journey through the colorful and artistic heart of Spain.

Unveiling Artisanal Gems in Tunisian Medina Markets

When your Mediterranean travels lead you to Tunisia, prepare to be captivated by the allure of the medina markets. These ancient marketplaces, often situated within the old town quarters, are a haven for those seeking unique handicrafts and local treasures.

Tunisia's medinas are famous for their handwoven textiles, intricately designed carpets, and exquisite leatherwork. As you meander through the narrow alleys, you'll find vibrant displays of vibrant fabrics, traditional clothing, and intricately embroidered linens. Don't miss the opportunity to witness skilled artisans at work, crafting leather bags, shoes, and accessories using techniques passed down through generations.

One of the standout souvenirs from Tunisia is the "fez" hat, a symbol of the country's heritage. Handmade and often decorated with intricate patterns, the fez is not just a stylish accessory but a piece of Tunisian history. Engaging with local sellers and craftsmen can offer insights into the cultural significance of these items, making your purchases all the more meaningful.

Captivating Capri: Cameos and Coral Jewelry

The stunning island of Capri in Italy is not only known for its breathtaking views but also for its exquisite coral jewelry and cameos. Wander through the narrow streets of Capri town and Anacapri, and you'll find charming shops offering these intricate pieces of wearable art.

Coral has been used in jewelry-making in Capri for centuries, and the vibrant red and pink hues are beautifully complemented by gold settings. Cameos, on the other hand, are delicate carvings usually made from shell or precious stones, depicting intricate scenes or profiles of famous figures. These timeless pieces capture the elegance and history of the island.

Exploring Spain's Alhambra and Al-Andalus Artistry

In Spain, the Alhambra in Granada stands as a testament to the stunning artistry of the Nasrid Dynasty. The intricate tilework, known as "azulejos," adorns the palace's walls, creating a mesmerizing mosaic of color and design. While you may not be able to take pieces of the Alhambra itself, you can find replicas and similar tilework in shops across Andalusia.

Additionally, Andalusia's rich history of craftsmanship is reflected in its leather goods, such as intricately carved leather bags and wallets. These items often feature designs inspired by the Islamic motifs that have left an indelible mark on the region's culture.

Unveiling Artistic Gems in Santorini's Studios

Santorini, the jewel of the Aegean, is known for its stunning sunsets, white-washed buildings, and crystal-clear waters. However, beyond its famous landscapes, the island harbors a thriving artistic community that produces unique souvenirs reflective of the island's beauty.

Wandering through the labyrinthine alleys of Santorini's towns, you'll encounter numerous art studios and galleries. Local artists draw inspiration from the island's colors and contours to create a wide range of artwork, from vivid paintings and sculptures to handcrafted jewelry and accessories. Don't hesitate to step into these studios and engage with the artists. They often share insights into their creative processes and the stories behind their pieces, adding depth to the art you bring back.

Consider investing in a piece that resonates with your experience of Santorini. It could be a seascape that captures the island's iconic blue-domed churches against the backdrop of the Mediterranean, or a handcrafted piece of jewelry adorned with locally sourced gemstones. These treasures will not only serve as tokens of your journey but also as windows into the island's thriving artistic scene.

Exploring Marrakech's Medina: Moroccan Craftsmanship

Venturing into the heart of Marrakech's historic Medina is like stepping into a time capsule of rich Moroccan culture and craftsmanship. The bustling souks here offer an array of souvenirs that capture the essence of Morocco's vibrant traditions.

Moroccan rugs, known for their intricate designs and vibrant colors, are a favorite among visitors. Each rug tells a story through its patterns and symbols, often representing the region where it was crafted. Rug shopping in the Medina is a fascinating experience, with merchants unfurling their treasures for you to admire.

The souks also offer a variety of handmade leather goods, from intricately designed bags and shoes to poufs and accessories. Moroccan leather is renowned for its quality, and you can even witness the tanning process at traditional tanneries in the city.

Additionally, the Medina is a treasure trove of lanterns, ceramics, and metalwork. The intricate latticework of Moroccan lanterns casts captivating patterns when illuminated, creating a mesmerizing atmosphere. Ceramics, often adorned with geometric patterns and vibrant colors, range from delicate teacups to ornate decorative plates.

As you explore the Medina, don't forget to engage with the local artisans. Many are passionate about sharing their craft and traditions with visitors, making your shopping experience a cultural exchange in itself. By collecting Moroccan crafts, you're not just taking home exquisite souvenirs but also preserving the legacy of generations of artisans.

Discovering Lace and Embroidery in the Greek Islands

The Greek islands are not only a paradise of sun and sea but also a hub of traditional crafts that celebrate the local heritage. One of the hidden gems you can uncover is the intricate lacework and embroidery that adorns textiles, clothing, and accessories.

Islands like Mykonos, Rhodes, and Crete are known for their skilled lace makers. Delicate lace, known as "kopaneli," is often handmade by local artisans and showcases intricate patterns inspired by the sea and nature. The technique involves weaving and knotting threads to create intricate designs that reflect the beauty of the islands.

Embroidery, too, holds a special place in Greek craftsmanship. You can find hand-embroidered linens, clothing, and decorative items adorned with colorful motifs. Each piece is a testament to the love and dedication invested by the artisans who meticulously create them.
When you acquire lace and embroidery souvenirs from the Greek islands, you're not just purchasing items of beauty, but also preserving traditions that have been passed down for generations. These pieces carry a sense of authenticity that connects you to the culture and artistry of the Mediterranean.

Ceramic Delights from the Islands of Greece

Greece's Mediterranean islands are renowned not only for their breathtaking scenery but also for their centuries-old tradition of ceramics. Each island has its distinct style and techniques, resulting in an array of beautifully crafted pieces that reflect the local culture and landscape.

Santorini, with its stunning caldera views, is known for its unique volcanic pottery. You'll find vases, plates, and ornaments adorned with swirling patterns and vibrant colors inspired by the island's geological history. Rhodes is celebrated for its decorative terracotta figurines and traditional "Rhodian plates," adorned with intricate blue and white designs.

The island of Crete is famous for its "kouros" and "kore" figurines, which harken back to ancient Greek art. These small sculptures often represent youthful figures and are a nod to the island's rich mythological heritage.

Collecting ceramics from the Greek islands not only adds a touch of Mediterranean elegance to your living space but also serves as a connection to the artistic legacy of these vibrant communities.

Browsing Antique Markets in Provence

While the Mediterranean's allure often conjures images of beaches and sun-drenched landscapes, the region also boasts its share of enchanting antique markets. In the picturesque towns of Provence, France, antique enthusiasts and collectors can find a wealth of treasures that span different eras and styles.

Stroll through markets like L'Isle-sur-la-Sorgue's Sunday Antique Market, where you'll uncover vintage jewelry, intricately designed furniture, and ornate mirrors. For those with a penchant for vintage fashion, the markets offer a selection of timeless clothing and accessories that carry the stories of decades past.

Antique markets in Provence are a delightful way to explore the region's history and craftsmanship. Each piece holds a story, and bringing one home means preserving a slice of Provencal heritage in your own living space.

Exploring Local Artistry Across the Mediterranean

Beyond Turkish bazaars and Andalusian ceramics, the Mediterranean region is brimming with a diverse range of local crafts waiting to be discovered. Consider the following experiences:

- Tunisian Textiles: Explore the intricate world of Tunisian textiles, including elaborately woven carpets and exquisite embroidered fabrics.

- Italian Leather Goods: Indulge in Italy's leather craftsmanship, from stylish bags and shoes to finely crafted accessories.

- Greek Jewelry: Discover the allure of Greek jewelry, with designs inspired by ancient motifs and contemporary flair.

- Moroccan Metalwork: Lose yourself in Morocco's medinas, where you can find intricate metal lanterns, mirrors, and tea sets.

- Spanish Flamenco Accessories: Immerse yourself in the vibrant culture of Spain by exploring Flamenco-inspired accessories, including ornate fans, elaborate hair combs, and hand-painted castanets.

- Cretan Embroidery: Experience the intricate embroidery of Crete, Greece, where traditional designs are meticulously woven into textiles like tablecloths, shawls, and clothing.

- Maltese Lace: Delve into the delicate art of Maltese lace-making, where fine threads are skillfully woven into intricate patterns on handkerchiefs, doilies, and clothing.

- Provencal Fabrics: Transport the charm of Provence, France, into your home with colorful fabrics adorned with classic Provencal designs, including sunflowers, lavender, and olive branches.

- Sicilian Ceramics: Explore the captivating world of Sicilian ceramics, known for their bright colors and intricate patterns. Discover plates, tiles, and decorative items adorned with unique Mediterranean motifs.

- Turkish Tea Sets: Bring a piece of Turkey's tea culture home with beautifully designed Turkish tea sets, including ornate teapots, delicate glasses, and decorative trays.

- Portuguese Azulejos Tiles: Capture the beauty of Portugal's iconic ceramic tiles, known as azulejos, by collecting hand-painted tiles featuring intricate geometric and floral patterns.

- Cyprus Lefkaritika Lace: Delve into the heritage of Cyprus with Lefkaritika lace, a traditional craft known for its exquisite needlework and delicate lace patterns.

- Egyptian Papyrus Art: Experience the allure of ancient Egypt by acquiring papyrus art featuring depictions of pharaohs, hieroglyphics, and scenes from Egyptian mythology.

- French Perfumes: Immerse yourself in the world of luxury French perfumes, available in a wide range of scents and elegantly designed bottles.

- Venetian Masks: Dive into the mysterious world of Venetian masquerade with elaborately crafted masks that evoke the enchantment of the Carnival of Venice.

- Balkan Pottery: Discover the rich pottery traditions of the Balkans, with hand-painted plates, bowls, and jugs that showcase the region's diverse cultural influences.

- Sardinian Basketry: Explore the intricate art of Sardinian basketry, where natural materials like straw and reeds are woven into beautiful baskets, bags, and household items.

- Lebanese Mosaic: Appreciate the skillful art of Lebanese mosaic-making, where colorful tiles are expertly arranged to create stunning patterns on decorative items and jewelry.

- Croatian Filigree: Admire the precision of Croatian filigree jewelry, characterized by delicate metalwork featuring intricate designs and motifs.

In conclusion, souvenir shopping in the Mediterranean goes beyond mere acquisition; it's a way to connect with the soul of a place. Unearthing artisanal treasures in Turkish bazaars and collecting ceramics and pottery from Andalusia provides a unique opportunity to bring home tangible pieces of the culture, creativity, and history that make the Mediterranean a truly enchanting destination. As you browse, bargain, and engage with local artisans, remember that each item you choose becomes a cherished link between your own story and the vibrant tapestry of the Mediterranean's past and present.

Conclusion

Reflecting on the Mediterranean Experience: Enduring Memories and Insights

As we reach the culmination of this journey through the pages of the "Mediterranean Travel Guide: Unveiling the Splendors of Sun-soaked Shores," it's time to pause and reflect on the captivating adventure that has unfolded. The Mediterranean, with its tapestry of cultures, landscapes, and history, has left an indelible mark on every traveler who has had the privilege to explore its shores.

Throughout this guide, we've embarked on a virtual odyssey, from the glamorous French Riviera to the ancient ruins of Ephesus in Turkey, from the architectural wonders of Alhambra in Spain to the hidden treasures of Greece's picturesque islands. The Mediterranean has offered a sensory feast, with its tantalizing cuisine, vibrant festivals, and breathtaking vistas.

As we consider the diverse cultures that intertwine along this vast coastline, it becomes clear that the Mediterranean is not just a geographical region; it's a confluence of histories, traditions, and stories. The chapter on culture and traditions unveiled the grandeur of Venice's Carnival, where masked figures dance through the narrow alleys, and the fervor of Spain's La Tomatina, where streets turn into a sea of red during this unique tomato-throwing festival. From the art of Florence's Renaissance to the culinary excellence of Greek mezze, every facet of the Mediterranean experience has woven a rich tapestry of human expression.

Practical travel tips have equipped us with the knowledge to navigate this vibrant mosaic with ease. Whether it's understanding visa requirements, packing for the diverse climates, or embracing various modes of transportation, these insights ensure that our journey remains seamless and enjoyable. Learning key phrases to connect with locals has further enriched our interactions, creating bridges between cultures that transcend language barriers.

Outdoor activities have invited us to engage with the Mediterranean's natural beauty actively. The azure waters have beckoned us to snorkel through Cyprus' Blue Lagoon and windsurf off the coast of Sicily. The mountains and trails have challenged us to explore hidden corners, from the Lycian Way in Turkey to Corsica's rugged landscapes. Each adventure has connected us with the environment and allowed us to appreciate the region's geographical diversity.

Delving into accommodation and local interactions, we've discovered the charm of boutique stays and the authenticity of homestays. These experiences offer not only comfortable lodgings but also opportunities to forge connections with the local way of life. From rustic farmstays to immersive cultural exchanges, these interactions have provided a genuine glimpse into the heart of Mediterranean communities.

As we conclude this guide, let us remember that the memories we've gathered along the Mediterranean's sun-soaked shores are more than just snapshots and souvenirs. They are a tapestry of experiences, a collection of encounters, and a mosaic of moments that have forever changed us. The Mediterranean is not merely a destination; it's a voyage of the soul, an exploration of the senses, and an education in the history of humankind.

So, whether you're reminiscing about a sunset captured in Santorini, savoring the flavors of Catalan tapas, or recalling the laughter shared with new friends in a Turkish bazaar, the Mediterranean's essence will continue to echo within you.

May the insights gained from this guide inspire you to continue exploring, learning, and cherishing the beauty that the world has to offer. As we bid adieu to the Mediterranean for now, remember that the memories we've gathered will forever be our North Star, guiding us toward new horizons and cherished experiences.

Made in United States
North Haven, CT
18 May 2024

52664767R00114